DAVE WOOD'S
CHRISTMAS BOOK

Stories, Traditions, Recipes, & Celebrations

A Compendium Gleaned
from 150 Years of His Family's Life
in the Upper Midwest

By Dave Wood
Former Minneapolis Star Tribune Columnist

Kirk House Publishers
Minneapolis, Minnesota

Dave Wood's Christmas Book
Stories, Traditions, Recipes, & Celebrations

A Compendium Gleaned from 150 Years of His Family's
Life in the Upper Midwest

By Dave Wood

Cover photo by Darlene Pfister Prois

Library of Congress Cataloging-in-Publication data
Wood, Dave, 1936
    [Christmas book]
  Dave Wood's Christmas book : stories, traditions, recipes, & cel-
ebrations, a compendium gleaned from 150 years of his family's life
in the upper midwest / by Dave Wood.
        p. cm.
    ISBN 1-886513-85-6 (alk. paper)
      1. Christmas--Middle West. 2. Christmas cookery--Middle West.
Middle West--Social life and customs. I. Title.
GT4986.M5W66 2003
394.2663'0977--dc22
                                                          2003058897

Kirk House Publishers, PO Box 390759, Minneapolis, MN 55439
Manufactured in the United States of America

For Ruth,
thanking her for her editorial savvy,
her unflagging support, and, most of all,
for helping me rediscover the joy of Christmas.

ACKNOWLEDGMENTS

Thanks to all the people who have come to our Christmas parties, have sung carols at our piano, have made our 34 years of Christmases together truly exciting. Thanks also to the accomplished writers who have seen fit to endorse this little effort.

Bob Burrows of the River Falls Journal made this book immeasurably better when he photographed several of the items that make our holidays special, as did our friends Livia Carlson and Grace Sulerud, whose cameras are always at the ready. Years ago, Darlene Pfister Prois of the Minneapolis Star Tribune sent me a photo of me playing Santa Claus at Dayton's downtown store. It graces the cover of this book. Finally, a special thanks goes to Leonard Flachman of Kirk House Publishers, whose expertise as a publisher made bringing this project to fruition a pleasure.

Dave Wood
River Falls, Wisconsin

TABLE OF CONTENTS

INTRODUCTION
or WARNING TO READER

If you are a disciple of Jan Schoenwetter's diet system, or

If you follow the advice of Jenny Craig, or

If you are on a low carbohydrate diet, or

If you're on the grapefruit diet, or

If you claim with a straight face that you prefer skim to whole milk, or

If you have recently purchased the new South Beach diet book, or

If you are still mourning the death of Dr. Atkins, who slipped on his own bacon grease,

Then close this book immediately and put it back on the shelf!

Nah, just kidding.

Even if you're a rabid dieter or conscious of responsible eating, this book can still be read with profit, can still be a lot of fun.

For one thing, it's not just about Christmas goodies, but ethnic customs in general.

For another, if you watch your calorie intake like a hawk, when you finish this book, you can feel very superior to my wife and me and our family and friends.

For still another, if your occupation happens to involve agriculture or grocery marketing, you'll be glad in the knowledge that there are still people out there who eat to their heart's content.

Finally, Christmas comes but once a year, and maybe this little book will inspire you to leave the diet for awhile and tread the primrose path of dalliance, take some time to smell the roses— AND the roast beef.   So jump in right now and listen to our tale.

CHAPTER ONE

DOING CHRISTMAS IN A BIG WAY

If you should put even a little on a little,
and should do this often,
soon this too would become big.
—Hesiod

For more than three decades my wife Ruth and I have celebrated Christmas as if there'd never be another one.

The celebration begins right after Thanksgiving, the church lutefisk supper season, when we travel to my hometown, Whitehall, Wisconsin, hear about how good the fish was at First Lutheran's church supper in Blair the night before, then buy a tree from my school pal, Gale Gabriel, a tree farmer. Once home, the tree goes up almost immediately and we decorate with great abandon and eccentricity.

Suddenly, our sisters and brothers and nieces and nephews appear in our collective consciousness after months of lying dormant, and the phone lines hum across the continent. We've always been churchgoers, but suddenly forthcoming church services, concerts and "doings" edge themselves toward the center stage of our household.

Sounds very aesthetic and spiritual, right?

Well, not quite right. It's also very physical.

For weeks we bake and we cook and we fill our freezer with edibles for the big party that usually occurs as soon as my wife escapes from her teaching duties for the holiday break.

We bake Russian tea cakes, cranberry bread and the white rye once baked in outdoor ovens by Polish ladies in Independence, Wisconsin, ladies who were closed down by food safety Nazis. I've managed to coax a recipe away from Mrs. Marge Pape of Independence and now bake it in my indoor oven ("Take 36 cups of flour...."). Ruth is an expert on toffee and peanut brittle and chocolate truffles and caramels, so boxes of those artery-cloggers begin to stack up wherever there's space. I make a Scandinavian specialty, Gravlax, which loosely translates as "salmon in a grave." Each year I also roll tiny meatballs, about 500 of them, pungent with Norwegian spices like cloves, poultry seasoning, and cardamom; then it's on to country pate, laced with brandy, thyme, and nutmeg. Jellied chicken is usually on the menu, as is potato lefse, a baking procedure we've never mastered as well as an outfit called Countryside, which bakes it in the little town of Blair, where I went to grade school.

A few days before the party, we race to Minneapolis for three essential stops. Ingebretsen's Scandinavian market on Lake Street where we purchase their homemade pickled herring, sylte (a veal head cheese), pultost ("young" cheese), lamb roll, and cured veal tongue. Then it's west to Bill's Mediterranean Market for feta cheese and Calamata olives and finally to Delmonico's in northeast Minneapolis for the Italian offerings. Long before the era of "inclusivity," we've been politically correct, always serving a huge antipasto of capicolla, Genoa salami, provolone cheese, roasted peppers, cured Italian olives. On the morning of the party, Ruth spends hours artfully arranging the huge platter, while I process the hummus and prepare the pita bread for the oven. We wouldn't think of letting the Lebanese and the Greeks down. What we have is what you might call a Multi-cultural Groaning Board.

We began this custom in Minneapolis in 1969, the year before we were married, my first year at Augsburg College, Ruth's at Robbinsdale Senior High. We invited the only people we knew in Minneapolis. Fifteen strong, we sat around the tree in my little apartment on Cedar Avenue and sipped and ate and sang the Tunes of Glory—"Good King Wenceslas," et al.

As our circle of friends grew, so did our party. These days about 100 people show up at our 120-year-old house in River Falls, Wisconsin, where Ruth teaches at the university (and where I have lots of retirement hours to roll meatballs and time to keep the old house from caving in).

And that's just the beginning. On Christmas Eve, it's always oyster stew (a bow to my Yankee ancestors) and rollepolse sandwiches (a bow to Martha, my Swedish grandmother). That's followed by a good bottle of Port and opening presents around the tree with my sister Kip and her husband and any other relatives who might be handy. Because we come from a racially mixed family—Yankee and Swede with a Norwegian stepmother thrown in— there's always talk about when we were kids, the Christmas pageant at the Norwegian Lutheran church in Whitehall, the disappointments under the tree and Uncle Olaf who came to Christmas Eve supper late, straight from Risberg's Bar on Main Street.

After one such session, I was inspired to write a poem in Scandinavian dialect for the old Minneapolis Tribune. After it appeared in the newspaper, I was asked for several years to read it on Christmas Eve day over WCCO-Radio on the late, lamented Charlie Boone and Roger Erickson show, a Twin Cities institution long gone and one I miss dearly. Here's my take on Clement Moore's "A Visit from St. Nicholas." It's written phonetically and meant to remind us of the way some of our older relatives used to murder English pronunciation. Read it very carefully because this might be your last chance. Years after the Tribune first published it, I asked my Star Tribune bosses if it could be published again. They told me no. It would be politically incorrect to print something in phonetic dialect because it made fun of the way an immigrant class used to speak English. So, at the risk of offending everyone, here it is. (Be sure to read it aloud, the way I've spelled it, to get the swing of it.)

A WISIT FROM ST. NICHOLAS

Vuss da nate before Chrissmuss, an' all trew da house,
Not ing-a-ting vusss stirring, not ee-wenn a mouse.
Da Jung funss vuss packed lake sardeence in vun bed
Vile wish-unss uff rommegrot danced in dare head.

Ma, she kewked lew-ta-fisk in a nightgown of puce.
And me? Ay yusst sucked on a big cud uff snoose.
Den oh-wer da hoghouse aroce such a cladder,
Ay yumped from da tee-wee tew see vhut vuss da madder.

Avay tew da front porch ay romped in may bewtss
Lake Ingvald, da hired man, on vun uff his tewtss.
Den vhut tew may vundering ice should appear?
A Yohn Deere corn binder, pulled by eight vite-tail deer.

Vid a little old drifer so nimble an' kvik,
Dat ay sviftly de-dewced dat he musst be St. Nick.
Fasster den Pug Lund, da vite-tailss day came,
An' he visseled and shouted and called dem by name:

"Now Astrid! Now Birgit! Now Rundvig an' Ragne!
On Torbjorn! On Torsten! On Ole an' Magne!
Pass da manure pile, get on da ball,
Speed tew da farmhouse and climb op da vall!"

An' den in a tah-vinkling ay heard on our rewf
Da prancing an' pawing uff each little hewf.

Ay vent tew da fireplace tew trow on a stick,
An' down trew da shimney slid yolly St. Nick.

Hiss eyes day vuss blue, hiss smile it ver sveet,
Hiss nose vuss bright red from tew much aquavit.
Hiss cap vuss from Monkey Vord, his bewts verr Sears' Best
An' hiss bundle uff gifts put his back tew da test:

A krumkake baker, for Inger, my vife.
For me, a Rappala fish-cleaning knife.
Ski poless for Sven (pluss a novel by Undset).
For Lena? Membership in Nordmann's Forbundet.

Nick didn't make small talk, tewk giftss from hiss sack,
Lake Hadacol for Grandma an' her miss-rub-bel hack.
A truss for poor Leroy, for Ingvald some schnapps,
An' for Ole a "fuzz-buster" tew vord off da copss.

He hitched op his trouserss, viped his noce on hiss sleeve,
Consulted hiss sked-yewll, said "Yee, ay gotta leef."
Den, laying hiss finger inside uff hiss lip,
Nick dug out vet snoose, den gafe it a flip.

He sprang tew da binder, tew da deer gafe a vissel!
An' avay day all flew, lake a Pershing Crewce missile.
Ay heard him giff holler, ass he drofe out uff sight,
"Ya, Glad Yule tew all, an' tew all a gewd night!"

*(Young readers—if they're still with me—should know that
"Pug Lund," a Rice Lake, Wisconsin, native, was a legendary
halfback for Minnesota's Golden Gophers, back when Bernie
Bierman was their coach and they were national champions.
Hadacol was a cough syrup made up largely of alcohol.
Nordmann's Forbundet is a Norwegian-American fraternal
insurance organization.)*

After church on Christmas morning and more Tunes of Glory, we return home to throw the ribeye roast in the oven, with Ruth mixing up another artery clogger, Yorkshire pudding, which includes my favorite Basic Food Groups, egg batter and grease, two of nature's most perfect foods. Then we wait for our guests to arrive for pre-dinner cocktails. And hors d'ouevres: more gravlax and Swedish meatballs, what else?

And then it's over for another year, except to drag the tree out onto the lawn, with needles flying everywhere and Ruth admonishing me to BE CAREFUL WITH THAT TREE!!

Then we collapse into separate heaps, swearing we'll never do a Christmas like that again. The first time we swore that was about twenty years ago.

The book you're about to read is a celebration of American diversity and how our family came a long way—in more ways than one—to celebrate the American Christmas. The next chapter will explain why the Wood family refused to celebrate Christmas and why they began celebrating once they arrived in Wisconsin. After that, Ruth's family adds a Germanic dimension to our celebration. Then comes a remembrance of Christmas trees we have known, followed by a discussion of Scandinavian customs and various Christmas entertainments we have enjoyed. Did I forget gift giving and receiving? Nope. Finally, we arrive at Christmas Eve and several traditional family recipes to make sure we all stay fat and sassy.

Oh, one more preview: Scattered through the book you'll find more than a dozen "recipe cards" gleaned from family and friends who hail from many walks of life and belief systems. Follow them and you can throw a party as much fun as ours. Bon Appetit! And if you're back on your diet, read 'em and weep.

CHAPTER TWO

GETTING THERE

As the long-forgotten peoples of the respective continents
rise and begin to reclaim their ancient heritage,
they will discover
the meaning of the lands of their ancestors.
—Vine Deloria, Jr.

H ow did Ruth and I arrive at such a state of wretched
excess?

A look back on my family for the past 133 years shows that the
prospects weren't too promising. My great-grandad, Dave
Wood, was a true-blue Yankee. His family came over on the
Winthrop Fleet in 1635 and settled Lynn, Massachusetts,
dissenters to the core. A few years later his ancestor John
Wood, whose house still stands, was thrown in the stocks for
refusing to baptize his infant children and then kicked out of the
town he founded. Dave's wife was Mary Parsons, whose
ancestors came over on the Mayflower.

By the 19th century, the Woods were living in Catarraugus
County, New York, but as that filled up, they restlessly moved
west. In 1856, when Dave was 16, he left his mother and ailing
father at a hotel in Columbus, Wisconsin, and headed to their
new property in Trempealeau County. Dave dug a hole in a

sidehill and lived there during the first winter and waited for his folks to catch up with him. Eventually, they settled on beautiful stretches of bottom land and raised wheat until the market went south in the 1870s, after which Dave converted to baling hay and shipping it to Chicago ("Ten Ton Guaranteed in Every Carload" said his stationery) to the horse-drawn streetcar company.

In 1869, Dave began keeping a diary. He recorded his comings and goings every day until he died in 1927. In the 1990s an antiquarian appraiser judged it the oldest and longest continuous farmer diary in the U.S. I found the diaries years earlier packed neatly in an old ammunition chest in what was once Dave's horse barn. Before donating it to the Wisconsin State Historical Society regional archives in Eau Claire, I read every word of it. Some of the entries puzzled me, especially his accounts of his early Christmases on the west central Wisconsin frontier. Here's a sample, with my own remarks in brackets.

December 25, 1869:
Fair & warm. Worked on some desks at the School house till noon. At home in the afternoon. Wrote to Mr. Coon of Otter Creek a letter to say I have money to pay on a note he holds against me. S. Doud [a cousin] & wife are here on a visit this afternoon.

What's going on here? It's Christmas Day and Dave is doing business? Is he some kind of Ebenezer Scrooge, or what?

December 25, 1872:
Cold & windy. Cut wood & got ready to go to town with wheat.

I asked the same question when I got to that entry. Later, I learned that religious dissenters like the Wood family rarely celebrated Christmas because, first, it wasn't mentioned in the Holy Bible, and second, the Anglicans, whom they detested, made a big deal out of the event. Just last year, Ruth and I made a pilgrimage to the Plymouth Colony "plantation" in Massachusetts, where actors are hired to play the roles of the first settlers. These kids know their onions and even speak in the dialect of the 17th century and never let down the façade of reality. We visited the dirt-floored home of William Bradford, from whom my great-grandma descends. Bradford wasn't there, but his aide was. Hoping to catch him in an error, I asked him how the colonials celebrated Christmas. He looked at me as though I had said a very bad word. He then replied that two years earlier, two Anglicans had made their way from England to the colony. When Christmas rolled around, they asked Governor Bradford if they could take the day off from their labors. Bradford said he personally didn't approve, but that he respected their right to worship in their own way and that if they wanted to they needn't go into the forest to cut wood. When the other pilgrims returned from their labors, the two Anglicans were drunk. "I think," said the aide, "that be enough said!"

December 20, 1873:
Fair & pleas. Took two loads of Wheat to Preston Depot [present-day Blair] and sold for 92 cts. Had on 122 bus. Recd $112.40. let Father have $5 & gave Mary five to get things for Christmas tree &c. Paid Mrs. Cook [maid] for work. Cash & articles furnished $14.55.

"Christmas tree &c," eh? What's going on now? Has Dave kicked his Baptist traces? That's what I first thought upon reading this entry. Then I went back through the previous two years and have come up with another theory. In his entries, Dave reports the arrival of new settlers. He calls them "Norskes" and "Polacks." I'm not certain, but I'd like to think when Dave and Mary saw the festive celebrations of their new neighbors, both from countries with strong holiday traditions, the Wood family eventually came around to celebrate another year of survival on the cold and sometimes grim frontier.

December 24, 1874:
Cloudy & cool. Frits [Sielaff, the German immigrant hired man] drawed wood & some posts & done chores in afternoon. I went to shop & got my horses shod 2.80. Took boys sled to get it ironed. Cost of same and to paint on sled $2.50. Went to Christmas tree in the evening at the M.E. [Methodist Episcopal] Church. Had a pleas. time.

"Methodist Episcopal"? Well, I'll be! Ecumenicism on the frontier. And the sled. Dave and Mary had two boys by now, Jim, age 7, and Archie, age 10. The very sled to which Dave refers reposed for a century in the horse barn where I discovered the diaries. It was a heavy homemade bobsled, painted a seriously faded red, and it had shiny steel attached to the bottoms of the bentwood runners. A few years ago, in shuffling through a tub of old photos, I found a picture of Jim and Archie aboard the sled, which was harnessed to a confused-looking shorthorn bull calf.

December 24, 1875:
Rained this mor & it has been a wet day. Went to the station & finished up the chairs at the church & got some things for Christmas. Gloves $2.50 & oysters & crackers 1.60. Apples 50. Lemmon extract .25

Oysters!! Now we're getting somewhere. And apples. According to Jane Peterson's recent book, "Between Memory and Reality" (University of Wisconsin Press), Dave's son Ralph, my grandpa, was the first Yankee in Lincoln township to marry a European immigrant's daughter. She was Martha Johnson, youngest daughter of Carl Johnson, a prosperous farmer from Osseo, Wisconsin. That was after he served in the Swedish merchant marine before jumping ship in New York harbor and walking all the way to LaCrosse before finding a job. Like the Woods, Carl was also a dissenter, this time from the Swedish Lutheran church. But he was no Baptist. He was an atheist. My grandmother remembers how Christmas was celebrated in her childhood home. She and her siblings would whine about all the other families going to church, etc. So the elder Johnson would parade the kids down into the cellar, wield a jackknife and give each kid half an apple. "On other days of the year," Grandma recalled, "we could eat all the apples we wanted."

December 25, 1879
Fair & Very cold 38 degrees below this mor... & it is 6 below to night. At home all day. Brought Grandma over & took her home again. Also cut & drew a little wood from here. Santaclaus brought me a shaving glass & cup. Also a watch case. He also remembered the rest of the family.

So after ten short years on the frontier, my Yankee family was celebrating Christmas. My vision of this hard-bitten great grandpa, who 23 years earlier had lived in a hole in the ground outside of present-day Whitehall, who walked 40 miles to La Crosse years back to carry a plow on his back to hitch to his only oxen had come to attend not only the Baptist, but the Methodist church, had eschewed some of his business dealings to buy gifts for his wife and kids and to entertain the idea that there was someone out there named "Santaclaus."

It obviously impressed his 12-year-old son Jim, who had been given a diary to keep the year before. Here's his account of Christmas 1879:

It is Christmas today. Ma got a pair of overshoes, some mittens, and a pincushion. Pa got a mug, a lookingglass, and a watch pocket. Archie got a toy wheelbarrow, a book, and some cloth for a shirt. I got a toy wheelbarrrow, a nice scarf, and a book. Mr. Tull gave Ralph a new pair of shoes.

Ralph. That's my grandpa, Ralph Winthrop (named after the 17th century immigrant fleet) Wood. He was born late, in 1879, when his mother was 40, and so the shoes he received from the community's shoemaker were probably rather tiny. In reading the diaries, I began to realize that Ralph would not have been, nor I here to record this family's story, except for a sad event that occurred in 1877, involving Dave and Mary's little children, Archie, Jim, Alta, and Kippy—and Janey, the hired girl. That year, just after Mr. Ellison's threshing rig pulled up to the Wood homestead, my great grandad reported to his diary that little Alta, age 2, had "signs of diphtheria." Within a week, all four kids and Janey the hired girl had come down with the dread disease. In two weeks, Alta, Kippy, and Janey were dead. The boys were older and survived.

It must have been a sad year for the family, without the sound of little voices echoing through the big house that Dave had built the year before. And lonely. About the time I discovered Dave's diaries, there burst upon the literary scene a bestseller, Michael Lesy's "Wisconsin Death Trip," which was later made into a movie and an opera composed by Conrad Susa. Lesy's book covered the same period the diaries covered in a place called Black River Falls, just 25 miles from Dave's homestead. I never much cared for Lesy's book, because whenever his characters got in trouble over by Black River Falls, they either went crazy and were sent to the mental hospital in Mendota or committed suicide or—my favorite—"died from grief." If you believe Lesy, Wisconsin pioneers were a pretty nutty lot. My great-grandparents were not nutty. When they lost offspring, they just went back to the matrimonial "workbench" and conceived another—my grandpa. They were some tough customers, as evidenced in Dave's business-like entries during the diphtheria epidemic. But they had their soft sides, as evidenced in this poem written by Mary, a former schoolmarm, after the birth of her youngest son. She called it "Baby's Hour":

> Ruddy arrows pierce the gloom
> Of this silent, dusky room,
> Airy currents woo my cheek
> And with many a wanton freak
> Lift my Berrie's shining hair

As I, with a measured motion,
Waft him in this easy chair.

And the long-forgotten tune,
That I whimsically croon,
Of a weird and ancient ditty,
Soothed him like a poppy potion,
Scarce five minutes gone, not more,
Since his quick, exploring eyes
Saw, with look of vague surprise,
The moonbeam trembling on the floor,
So frail and wan, he had no doubt
His scanty breath might blow it out.

A shadow shifting over head
Like some dark bird with wings outspread,
And images grotesque and queer
That from the mirror mock and leer.
But now the lids begin to drop
As though they needed each a prop,
Winking slow, and winking slower,
Ah! My Berrie, what a pity,
In a world so full of sights,
Little eyes need shut of nights.

Now I press him to my heart,
With a sudden, tender start,
Little one with breath of balm,
May your slumber be as calm
When the years have slipped away,
When you're old and worn and gray,
And the puzzle and the kinks
Of lights and shadows which methinks
Vex your weak and weary brain,
To your wiser sight grow plain;
Seem then to your thoughtful gaze,
Types of life's bewildering ways.
Sleep my Berrie, now no care
Wakes you e'er to plaint, or prayer.

My Grandpa grew up in a bewildering world, but he never turned gray. And he celebrated Christmas with all the enthusiasm and generosity he could muster. Those are stories for a later chapter.

But I digress. When Christmas rolled around the year of the epidemic, little Jim and his older brother Archie, the survivors, enjoyed a very generous visit from "Santaclaus": Each received a new Sunday suit and scads of stockings and mittens. A wagon for Jim, a rifle for Archie, age 13. And the tradition of gift-giving continued in the Wood family. Our home library has an entire section devoted to books from Ralph's youthful bookshelf, almost all of them Christmas gifts from his parents. Several Horatio Alger novels, as well as "Girl of the Limberlost," "Rebecca of Sunnybrook Farm," "Aylmer's Folly," and my all-time favorite, "The Battleship Boys in Foreign Service." More about that later.

Ralph grew up and took his aforementioned Swedish-American bride, who brought an Old World cuisine along with her to the banks of the Trempealeau. Ralph pitched right in. Here was a Yankee, 6 feet tall, 160 pounds dripping wet, who could eat blodklub, gammelost, lutefisk, lefse, and rollepolse with the most eminent Scandinavian trenchermen—make that trencherpersons—in the valley. "I'm so skinny," he'd say, "because I lose weight carrying around all this digesting food."

He also heartily approved his father-in-law's attitude toward religion and never went to church. Furthermore, he was partial to the Scandinavian attitude toward alcoholic beverages, which was more positive than that of his own family. When I was a boy, Christmas always sent him to Roy Fortun's drugstore to purchase a bottle of 190 proof grain alcohol from which he concocted a fabulous punch (See recipe in Chapter Nine). I never saw him tipsy, but occasionally he was happy, which is more than you can say for most Yankees.

And Grandma? She came from a very rustic hill family. But she quickly adapted to "urban" living near the county seat. She also took to foods that were brand new to her with a convert's gusto. Like lettuce. And sweet corn. When she discovered chow mein, it almost spelled the end of our Yankee/ Scandy holiday dinners. One year, she served chow mein at Thanksgiving. As we went home from that one, my father wondered aloud if there'd be the usual oyster stew on Christmas Eve. Grandpa for once in his life apparently put his foot down, and the cream and oysters bubbled on the old Beaver Dam cook stove again that year.

Clearly the family gatherings of my childhood set the patterns for a riot of mixed ethnicity in the years to come.

CHAPTER THREE

THE GERMAN INVASION

Let us put Germany in the saddle, so to speak
—it already knows how to ride.
—Otto von Bismarck

And what of Ruth's family? Her family records don't go back as far as mine, but when I joined the family in 1969, there was plenty of evidence that Christmas was alive and well at the home of my mother-in-law, Elsie Pirsig, nee Schwarz. Both of Elsie's parents came over from Feuchtwangen, Germany, in the early part of the twentieth century. They settled in an Iowa town on the Minnesota border called New Germania.

New Germania agreed to change its name in 1917, the year after Elsie's birth, due to an outbreak of Kaiserphobia, when the U.S. went to war with Old Germania. The city fathers changed its name to Lakota. To my knowledge, no Native-Americans moved back to the little town plunked down in the middle of the universe's largest soybean patch. And the Germans stayed, attended the Lutheran church and carried on many of the traditions brought over from the old country. Ruth's paternal grandmother was Wilhelmina Pirsig of Blue Earth and Elmore, so you can bet that she wasn't an Arab terrorist. Like Grandma Schwarz, Wilhelmina brought her German baking skills to bear on the upper midwest, garnering a raft of blue ribbons at the

Minnesota State Fair and stuffing cookies down her grandkids' gullets every Yuletide.

Elsie moved to an Italian suburb south of Chicago in 1950 and brought her Teutonic recipes with her. As soon as she came home from her factory job, she baked and baked for weeks on end in preparation for the holiday season. And she never forgot church, attending the little Lutheran mission church, surrounded by Roman Catholic cathedrals, fortune tellers on every corner, and Genoa salami.

A single mother of three young kids, new to a strange city, possessed of a tenuous factory job, Elsie survived because she carried with her the skills of economy her German parents instilled in her back in Lakota. Elsie counted the cookies in the cookie jar. The kids could have one each when they arrived home from school. And one peanut butter sandwich. Try to sneak another slice of bread and Elsie knew it when she got home from the factory.

Soon after Thanksgiving, Elsie spent her evenings baking goodies, because Christmas was on its way, from the least expensive ingredients, like sugar, water, and flour. Sure, from necessity Elsie was stern, and Elsie counted cookies throughout the year. But Christmas was different, when Elsie went the extra mile for her fatherless kids. Popcorn balls were cheap and the kids loved them. So after a hard day inspecting aerosol tops at National Can Corporation, Elsie scalded her tired hands making hot popcorn balls, and for a special treat ladled out scarce money for salted-in-the shell peanuts. "We had popcorn once in awhile, when it wasn't Christmas," Ruth recalls, "Never salted-in-the-shell peanuts."

And when Christmas rolled around, she laid out her culinary handiwork for the kids to enjoy. For the twelve days of Christmas there was no cookie counting. The kids could have all they wanted.

You never saw much Genoa salami around Elsie's house. Her bow to the Spice Islands was a Christmas delicacy called "Pfefferneuse," or pepper nuts. How to describe Pfefferneuse? They were like tiny jawbreakers made of flour, sugar, and of course, pepper. Elsie painstakingly rolled the dough into dime-sized cannonballs, baked them, and stored them in Mason jars for the onslaught of kids and grandkids, who loved them. If truth be told (and I can do so now, as Elsie died last fall) I never cared much for her Pfefferneuse. I much preferred the ones made by her kid brother Clarence Schwarz of Glencoe, Minnesota. His weren't quite as molar-smashing, were sweeter, and contained more pepper.

Once better times came, Elsie continued the tradition. On each Christmas Eve, we headed for the Sunday School program at the little German Lutheran church. Sitting on the hard pews, I thought of Grandpa and the alcohol punch and how much I missed both. But I loved that little church, too, because it had taken care of my wife and her hard-up and fatherless family when they were all alone in the new big city. Ruth remembers the Sunday school programs when she was a little girl. "They gave each of us kids a half-pound box of Fanny Farmer candies. I'd never seen anything so elegant."

Church was followed by Pfefferneuse. In the morning it was back to church and then home to an absolutely huge meal. Lutheran poet and theologian Gracia Grindal refers in one of her poems to her mother's "properly overcooked Lutheran beef roast." Elsie had that one down, too. It was dark brown and toothsome, cooked to an inch of its owner's well-developed musculature, the resultant gravy almost black. Black gold it was on her excellent mashed potatoes. Then more Pfefferneuse, three choices of pie, an incredible ice cream dessert, and hours and hours and hours and hours of card-playing. Apparently, if you don't drink hot alcohol punch, you've got to do something to while the time away.

We miss Elsie terribly. Last fall, at 85, she dug her onions and potatoes, rubbed the dirt off them, put them in containers in the pantry just as if she were still living in New Germania/Lakota. And then she died, quiet and dignified to the end. I figure she's the last citizen in Oak Lawn, Illinois, to know that onions and potatoes come out of the ground and are not dropped from the sky in orange mesh sacks. More of Elsie later.

CHAPTER IV

O, TANNENBAUM

The Admiral says that he never beheld so fair a thing:
Trees all along, beautiful and green,
and different from ours, with flowers and fruits,
each according to their kind.
—Christopher Columbus

Until just a few years ago, my father kept Christmas decorations in an old leather suitcase. I looked into it once when he was putting the remaining shards of "icicles," now banned, on his tree. I looked in and felt a big tug on my heartstrings. At the bottom of the valise were broken bits of popcorn, little circles of candle wax, a tiny clip-on candle holder and an incredibly ugly ornament.

The Christmas trees of my youth were something less than elaborate. I figure they were pretty much the same as the first ones Great Grandad Dave Wood cut when he decided to forget about the Bible and follow suit with his Polish and Norwegian neighbors. When I was a kid on the farm, it began with my dad trudging up the hill through the snow to the woodlot. He'd cut down a little long-needled evergreen and drag it down to the porch. Then he'd look in the woodpile for a big chuck of firewood that had been split in half. He evened off the split side with a double-bitted axe. On the arced side he got his big hand auger and ground a hole in the center. Into the hole he stuck the butt of the tree and dragged it into the living room. And then he went out into the barn to shovel cow shit.

Now it was mother's turn—and mine too. She loved decorations, but there wasn't much to hang on the tree. Moves from city to farm to farm to farm had resulted in many broken tinsel balls. Lights had burned out, and during World War II, replacements were hard to come by. Undaunted, she put me to work cutting strips of colored construction paper which, with the help of homemade paste, turned into colorful chains. She popped corn and we strung the popped kernels with a needle and thread and they became long strands of "snow." One year, she read that if you took some Lux laundry soap, added water and whipped it up with an egg beater, you could dab the resultant fluff on tree branches for more "snow"— in this case "drifts." She did it.

An unqualified failure.

The most tedious project had to do with candles. She resurrected several stubs of colored wax candle from the junk drawer. Lighting one at a time, she'd hand me the candle and I would let molten droplets land on our oilcloth-covered kitchen table. When the droplets, about one-third inch across, had hardened, my job was to scrape them off the oilcloth with a spatula and thread them into chains with a sharp needle and thread.

The first farm my father sharecropped on had no electricity, so modern lights were impossible; by the time we got to the second one, our Christmas lights were burned out and broken. That didn't stop my mother. Once the tree was festooned with paper circles, paraffin ropes, and popcorn, we gathered around the tree in the parlor, across from the potbellied stove in the corner. She produced a little candle in a holder with a clip-on, an artifact she had gleaned from her mother's belongings. She clipped the holder to a tree branch and gingerly lit the candle with a farmer match. We watched the candle flicker for five minutes—and then she carefully blew it out, amidst stories from my father about whole churches burning down during his youth because trees caught fire. When I think back, that five-minute flame was more exciting than all the crazy twinkly fixtures we have today and take for granted.

One December day in 1944, my mother read in the Blair Press that there were new Christmas tree decorations for sale at Stumpf's Store. My mother didn't drive, and my father was too busy helping out a neighbor. So she bundled up us kids and dragged us three miles to town on foot. We stomped our boots on the oiled wood floor of Stumpf's and headed for the decorations. Pitiful decorations they were. With all the rationing restrictions, manufacturers had to make do with no metal. My mother sighed and bought half a dozen cardboard balls, which had been covered with a matte finish ersatz aluminum foil. We trudged home and they found prominent places alongside the strands of popcorn.

That was my mother's last Christmas, for she died on her birthday the following February, at age 34, of a cerebral hemorrhage. When I looked again in that old suitcase, I saw the popcorn, saw the wax, saw the pitiful ornaments and memories of the needles, the thread, the candles, with my mother, popping corn came back to me. All that tedium was worth it because I was spending precious last moments with her that might not have been spent in easier times, when factory-made decorations were available.

When I married Ruth in 1970, I didn't realize that the Christmas tree decorations she would introduce to my life were much more bizarre than any amount of invention my mother had dreamed up.

It all began one night when we dined out at Harry's, that great Minneapolis eatery, long ago burned down. For whatever reason, we felt flush and ordered lobster tails. When we were wiping the last of the melted butter from our chops, Ruth looked down at the empty shells and said, "My, but they're beautiful!" When the waitress arrived with the check, Ruth asked for a doggy bag, swept up the shells, took them home, and boiled them to remove all shards of meat. Before Christmas, she shellacked them and up they went on our first Christmas tree. That began the tradition of hanging everything on the tree but the kitchen sink, which we would also hang, but Fraser firs' branches are much too delicate. While researching my family's history, I found a gaggle of tintype portraits of my ancestors, already framed in ornate golden borders. I attached hangers fashioned from paper clips and up they went. Mussel shells? Ruth asked for a doggy bag and spray painted them gold. Beautiful!

That's what people say when they come to our Christmas party. Of course, we use conventional tinsel balls, strands of beads, and old-fashioned lights inherited from relatives. But Christmas guests are always attracted to the offbeat stuff, like six miniature tubas purchased by Ruth in honor of my misspent musical career. So now when they come to the party, they bring all manner of fancy decorations, hand embroidered stars that we have to restarch every decade or so, Mexican straw ornaments, several little pillows embroidered by our friend, former Star Tribune Food Editor Mary Hart. Today we now have ten storage boxes of ornaments, a far cry from my family's old leather suitcase.

At one party, novelist Louise Erdrich came with her father Ralph in tow. Ralph, a retired teacher from Wahpeton, N.D., was fascinated by some of the decorations and commented about some of the more bizarre items.

"Still not as bizarre as the decorations my mother used when we were kids," replied Ruth.

Thereby hung a tale and Ruth was off and telling.

She was a very little girl when her family moved from Blue Earth, Minnesota, to a Chicago suburb to make their fortune. It didn't turn out that way, because her father left them with little more than a big mortgage on a little house, three kids in grade school, and a young wife with a high school education.

Fortunately, Elsie Pirsig had a job at National Can, where she worked on the line. But then her union went on strike, something new in the lexicon of the young woman from Blue Earth. The union benefits didn't cover expenses, to say nothing of Christmas, which was coming up. What would she do for a tree, and even for decorations since theirs had been left behind in Blue Earth?

She would lie, that's what.

Elsie left the picket line and broke the rules and went over to the local S.O.S. company, the outfit that manufactured those cute little plastic scrubbers—called "Tuffies"—that cut the crud off frying pans. She lied and said she was out of work and wanted a job. They gave her the job, also on the line. Things began to look up. She purchased a tree for $2.00. But there was also the matter of the ornaments. On Christmas Eve day, she came home from work toting two huge paper sacks.

Inside were more Tuffies, in every color of the rainbow, than could be imagined. God bless us, every one! That night the uprooted family decorated the tree with Tuffies and enjoyed a merry Christmas, despite their tribulations.

"Great story," said Ralph Erdrich, a talented writer in his own right.

About eleven months later there arrived in the mail a package from Wahpeton, North Dakota, from "R. Erdrich." We opened it to find—guess what—a blue Tuffy. It now graces our tree every Christmas.

CHAPTER FIVE

THE ETHNIC RENAISSANCE

Be fruitful and multiply, and replenish the earth,
and subdue it: and have dominion over the fish of the sea.
—Genesis, 1:28

When I arrived in Minneapolis at Augsburg College in 1969 after years in the groves of academe of the lower midwest, I had pretty much forgotten my Norwegian connections. But once there I was abruptly reminded, because first and foremost, Augsburg was a Norwegian-American college with deep Lutheran roots.

One of my new acquaintances was physicist Kermit Paulson. One day in the faculty lounge, he said he was leaving his young family that night to go home to Clayton, Wisconsin, where his parents' church was throwing a lutefisk supper up on the hill a few miles from the family farm. Could I go along? You bet. Lots of memories came flooding back once I got to Moe Church. Kerm and I dined vastly on the slippery stuff, and we left next morning with the sounds of Norwegian-America still ringing in our ears.

Those weren't the last uff-das we heard over the next several years. The ethnic revival was in full swing. Cultural commentator Michael Novak had recently declared that the ethnic melting pot was "unmeltable," that various nationalities who had migrated to the U.S. had managed to retain their identities, and good for them! That was good news to lots of south Minneapolitans, who celebrated their heritage as never before. One of the beneficiaries was Ingebretsen's Market on Lake Street, a century-old institution that began selling Scandinavian groceries out of necessity and continued to do it for the sake of nostalgia—and also because Scandinavian groceries tasted good. As I mentioned in Chapter One, at Ingebretsen's you could buy anything from canned fish balls to pickled ham; from sylte (both pan and loaf style), pultost (young cheese), veal tongue, and blood sausage to Swedish sausage and hand-rolled lefse made by little old ladies in the basement. One Christmas I ran into ex-governor Karl Rolvaag, who had driven from his retirement home up by Grand Rapids, Minnesota, just to come down and buy half a dozen tubes of cod roe, fish eggs that resemble pink toothpaste when you squeeze the tube. They're a fixture in Ingebretsen's fridge case, as is gjetost, a goat cheese that resembles petrified peanut butter or something even less pleasant than that, if you get my drift. Ruth, who had never eaten Scandinavian prepared meats before we discovered Ingebretsen's, is especially partial to the colorful and exotically spiced lamb roll, a sandwich meat that has become a centerpiece of our annual Christmas party.

One year, I was at Ingebretsen's to buy a sackful of party groceries. Ten butchers were on duty to serve the holiday trade. I took my number—99—and waited expectantly because I heard Bud Ingebretsen, whose father founded the place, call out 65. Only 34 to go, thought I. Finally, my number was called and I stepped up only to have co-owner Warren Dahl tell me that I was "in the second series," but that I had only 100 more to wait. A sweet little old lady stepped up to the counter and asked Warren, "Can you cook lutefisk in a microwave oven?"

"I don't know why not," replied Warren, a handsome fellow, ruddy as all get-out. "Folks cook other fish in microwaves. Of course there's a drawback. Once you cooked a piece of lutefisk in it, you'd have to throw the microwave away."

What passes for laughter in Norwegian-America rippled through the busy store.

Ingebretsen's is a store to which I continued to return long after leaving Augsburg, sometimes as a customer, sometimes as a feature writer for the Minneapolis Star Tribune. When I became book review editor at the newspaper, I began the custom of writing each December a send-up of some famous Christmas story with allusions to present-day Minneapolis. The first year, I featured Ingebretsen's in a spoof of Charles Dickens's "A Christmas Carol." Some of the allusions are a bit dated, but lots of folks got a bang out of it, and one suburban teacher even used it in her English class, so here it is.

It was the best of torsk, it was the worst of torsk.

That was what the estimable Bob Cratquist surmised as he chatted merrily with hundreds of other Minneapolitans at the counter of Ingebretsen's Market on Lake Street. The best, Bob thought, because each fillet was shim- mery-flaky and snow white, like the caps on Lake Hiawatha this chilly evening before Christmas morn. His youngest son was perched on Bob's humble right shoul- der, gazing in wonderment at the array of meat and fish lined up in holiday regiments, with a battalion of butch- ers behind them.

"Lewk, oh, lewk, fodder, lewk," exclaimed Tiny Torvald, pointing his frail little finger at the glass case. "Blood sausage, and salt herring!"

Ah, yes, there was blood sausage black as night, salt herring that would turn Lake Nokomis into a briny ocean, pigs' feet that seemed to say "I want to trot home beside

you and jump into a bubbly kettle." There was spicy
sylte and soft lefse and krumkake, crisp as a December
morn at the Cedar and Lake bus stop. And there was
torsk. The worst of torsk, thought Bob, because it cost
$2.95 the pound, twice his hourly clerk's wage at Scrod
& Marlberg's overshoe factory on the near north side.
And how long would that position last? wondered the
merry little clerk. His employer, Ebenezer Scrod, was a
Bostonian with an Ivy League background, and poor
Bob had only his Roosevelt High diploma to show when
the summer cutbacks came.

"Oh, fodder, fodder, can vee haf torsk?" implored Tiny
Torvald.

And so it was that Bob Cratquist ordered one fillet of
torsk for Christmas Day feasting. There was no turning
down Tiny Torvald, for the plucky little lad was gravely
ill and the Cratquist family knew not how many Christmases he had before him. For you see, gentle reader,
almost all the enamel had vanished from Tiny Torvald's
teeth because of his meager diet of cookies dunked in
coffee, and it had become oh-so-difficult to chew for
the sprightly little imp, and malnutrition was a wolf at
his life's door. Out into the cold of Lake Street Bob
hopped, after which Tiny Torvald shouted from his shoul-
der the oft-heard greeting, "God blass uss eh-worry vun!"

Lake Street was lit up, and so were some of its deni-
zens, as Bob gave his favorite offspring a horsy-back
ride through the drifts. They turned left on Cedar and
made their way to the family's modest but tidy apartment in Cedar Square West. The tiny abode was chilly,
but the family's warm feelings toward each other made
up for that a thousand fold, nay, more.

Mrs. Cratqist exclaimed, "Oh, may, may! Yew got torsk.
Vell issn't dat vunnerful?"

"I hope dare'ss plenty for all six uf uss," Bob ventured.

"Oh, oh. A whole pound? More dan enuf," said his cheerful spouse. "Vee got lefse tew. An' kewkies. An' yew can make some lemon an' yin punch. Ay tewk may ironing money an' bought uss a pint uff Fleischmann's Yin at da Wiking Bar on Ri-werside Ah-wa-noo."

It would be a wonderful Christmas, thought Bob, who could never be gloomy for more than a second. (Some thought Bob might not be 100 percent Norwegian because his outlook was ever-cheerful.)

"Capital," exclaimed Bob, who frolicked with Peder and Marta and the rest of his brood, unmindful for the moment of Ebenezer Scrod's shabby treatment of the Santa Anonymous people (of the overshoe factory) that very afternoon of the inescapable fact that his employer was a hard man, harder than a slab of lutefisk before its immersion in a tub of water and lye, before that final baptism by butter, a commodity the Cratquists could ill afford.

And then it was back down to Cedar Avenue with the torsk, which was to be baked at the New Riverside Café, because, to the Cratquists' soon-forgotten dismay, the gas had been turned off at Cedar Square West. Bob was in arrears with Minnegasco.

$\ast\ast\ast\ast\ast$

Out on Park Avenue in an old mansion that looked like a new mortuary, Ebenezer Scrod was having a difficult night of it. He'd no more than gotten his coat off and a Banquet pot pie into the microwave when the ghost of his late partner Jake Marlberg had tracked snow into the foyer. Marlberg had muttered something about Scrod, made mention of some late-night visitors, then walked through the closed door out into the mists and was gone.

"Bah, humbug," said Scrod, who was a man of few words and fewer emotions.

But then came the Ghost of Christmas Past, who swept Scrod back to his unhappy days at Harvard, back to his brief romantic interlude with the light of his life, a Smith girl with yellow tresses who finally bade him adieu when the young man became embroiled in the four buckle-three buckle controversy that rocked the overshoe world a half century ago. Scrod's tears flowed freely like Minnehaha Falls after the first Spring thaw.

Suddenly, he was back in Minnesota, with the Ghost of Christmas Present, who floated him along the ceiling at the St. Olaf College Christmas Concert, where the strains of "Beautiful Savior" wafted across his crusty old consciousness. Then it was on to Dayton's Auditorium and the annual Christmas display, then for a peek into his nephew Dick's modest home in the Seward Neighborhood, where Christmas Eve festivities were in progress. Dick was a Columbia Law School graduate who had refused a position at the overshoe company and worked, gratis, as the North Country Food Co-op's legal counsel. He and his friends were merrily playing Baby Boomers Trivial Pursuit and drinking mugs of hot organic apple cider garnished with mung beansprouts.

Finally, it was across the freeway to the cramped Cratquist apartment, where the humble family was merrily playing Rook, which did not require devilish face cards, and sucking the gelatin off the torsk bones and the last gin out of the lemon peels at the bottom of the punch pitcher. Suddenly, as if he were assaulted by a Minnesota snowstorm in April, Ebenezer Scrod realized that life was more than chasing Tribune columnist George Grimm and the other Santa Anonymous people out of his office. Suddenly, he began to clap his liver-spotted hands. Suddenly, he realized that Christmas was a time for love and good cheer and for God's blessing every one.

But then, but then, then came the Ghost of Christmas Yet to Come. Ebenezer Scrod was not a little displeased to find himself at a Welander-Quist-Davies funeral home. He and the Ghost were the only figures at the wake for a frail figure wrapped in a shroud from the woolen mills in Winona.

"Who," asked Scrod of the Ghost, "has passed from this mortal coil on the very, very best of all days of the year? And why has no one come for coffee and cookies? And why," he continued, "are the people out on Lowry Avenue so very, very merry, when they have hitherto been moved to tears for one of their fallen?"

The Ghost of Christmas Yet to Come replied, "The person in the shroud, Ebenezer Scrod, is YOU! YOU, Ebenezer Scrod. If you do not wish to have your goose cooked, finally, in an ignominious manner, you must change your ways. You must honor Christmas in your heart all the year." That said, the Ghost disappeared into the last spiral of the mourner's book, which was still empty.

● ● ●

Christmas Day dawned bright and clear with a windchill factor of minus 84. Ebenezer Scrod kicked off the covers after his nightmarish Christmas Eve, dressed quickly, put on his rubberized Scrod-Weejuns and tromped out onto the Avenue. He bounced south on Park toward Lake like a pop fly hit into the Metrodome's outfield, greeting people as he went with a hearty "Hasen gar det?" in the tongue of his adopted state, that is to say "How goes it?" Turning west on Lake, he came to Ingebretsen's Market and pounded mightily on the door, which was locked.

Ebenezer fired off a verbal fusillade that would have put the mock regiments at Fort Snelling to shame. Finally Warren Dahl came to the door and let the old man in, wondering what this stranger was doing at his establishment on Christmas morn.

"And what will it be for you, my good man?" aked Dahl, wrapping up a pound of odoriforous gammel ost for his own family's afternoon tea.

"What will it be for ME? Nay, nay, my good man. Not for me, not for me," said Scrod with a twinkle in his eye.

"Then for whom?" asked the jolly butcher, his cheeks a fiery red.

"For whom? For whom? For the finest family, the kindest family, the merriest family, the best family in all of this town! For the Cratquist family, my good man, the Cratquist family!"

"And what will it be?" asked Dahl. "Perhaps a fine leg of dried mutton, hard as a rock, the best we have?"

"That won't do," cried Scrod with some measure of sadness, remembering his ghostly visit of the previous eve and how Tiny Torvald had to swallow his torsk whole for lack of tooth enamel.

"Perhaps some lutefisk? "

"AHA! The very thing, a barrel of it—no—two barrels! And ten pounds of your finest melted butter, which should help it slide down little Torvald's gullet without benefit of mastication. Deliver it to Cedar Square West and you can blow your nose on this," said Scrod, tossing a gnarled fistful of legal tender on the counter, a munificent gratuity. "Now hail me a cab! I'm going to visit my nephew, Dick, that dear, dear boy, and send free overshoes to all those lovely young people who work at the North County Co-op."

EPILOGUE: And so it went on that memorable Christmas Day, which was by no means the end of our tale.

Ebenezer Scrod honored the spirit of Christmas all the year. He employed the city's finest orthodontist to heal Tiny Torvald. He promoted Bob Cratquist to factory ombudsman to adjudicate any employee complaint, however trivial. He gave ten percent of his pre-tax earnings to the Loft Writers' Workshop and the West Bank School of Music. And, from that time forward, he was a frequent guest of Torsk Klubben, the Norwegian fish-eating club. (He could not belong, however, because of his ancestry.) When Bud Ingebretsen invited him to join the rival Saga Klubben, which welcomed all nationalities, Ebenezer could not have been more pleased. Of course, it interfered with his puritan policy of total abstinence from spirits of either a liquid or chain-clanking nature, which was a far, far better thing he did than he had ever done before.

CHAPTER SIX

CHRISTMAS SEASON ENTERTAINMENTS

For I dance
And drink and sing
Till some blind hand
Shall brush my wing.
—William Blake

SINGING CAREER STYMIED AT EARLY AGE

After my mother died, I first lived with my Aunt Wylis, then settled in with Grandma and Grandpa Wood in the big house on Scranton Street. The war was still raging in the Pacific and so my cousin Billy Steig and Aunt Alma had taken up residence in the "Grandmother Apartment" vacated by the death of my great-grandma in 1935. Billy's dad was a career army officer stationed in the Pacific, and we waited anxiously for his letters, many of which had been mysteriously snipped into doilies by overzealous censors. Once we knew for sure he was in Borneo, because he wrote Aunt Alma that he was living with a lot of "wild men."

Billy and I also anxiously awaited the big Christmas concert at Our Saviour's Lutheran Church. Grandma and Grandpa did not attend church, but Grandma said if I was going to survive in Whitehall, I'd better start going to Sunday School and church and play ball with the mainstream. Evangelism, it seems, takes many forms and enlists many different people. I loved both activities, and Sunday School, of course, led to the church's Junior Choir. Billy and I joined in the fall of 1945. Rehearsals were held each Saturday morning. We trudged off each Saturday through the bright, crisp autumn air, while the other kids on Scranton Street were organizing touch football games or having pickle fights at the open air vats of the Onalaska Canning Company along the Green Bay & Western tracks.

Usually, Billy and I would climb up onto the pickle station ramp, pee in one of the vats full of curing cucumbers and then head for Our Saviour's. The rest of the guys could play all the football they wanted. We were ARTISTES. We'd be up front on the concert night, after which Santa Claus would pass out brown paper bags of candy. We'd be wearing gowns, with big red bows. We'd sing our hearts out.

Mrs. Blanche Ivers was our choir director. A wonderful woman, she was a bit younger than my parents and was especially solicitous of me, the poor motherless little boy. After two rehearsals, Mrs. Ivers passed out patterns for our new choir gowns, and we passed them on to my churchless grandma, who sat right down at the treadle-operated Singer and ran them up. Practices intensified, and when Bergie and Worm and Bear-puss were skiing at Allen Hill, we were heading through the pickle vats—now pumped empty—and singing our hearts out in front of the Cradle Roll and yellowed maps of the Holy Land in the very warm basement of Our Saviour's.

Finally, the big night arrived. Grandma put on her plush overcoat, Grandpa his old gabardine suit. My father took Aunt Alma by the arm and we walked through a light dusting of new snow to the Christmas Concert. We left our churchless elders behind—hoping they could find the nave—and went down to put on our gowns along with the high school choir and the real choir of adults. My father always called the males in the back row "The Holy Boys." But tonight he'd have to listen to them because he wanted to hear his own son belt out "Away in the Manger." Mrs. Ivers passed out candles that would be lit for a short interval while we marched to our pews. She cautioned us to be VERY careful and said that entire churches had been burned down by careless junior choir members of the past, whole congregations of people going up in smoke along with the building, the tree, etc, etc. As performance time approached, the tension was enormous. One girl threw up on her gown. Another had a messy nose bleed, apparently provoked by sheer terror. Billy and I were cool.

We marched in to the strains of Mrs. Louise Johnson on the pipe organ. The Junior Choir went first. We rose from our pews and took our places before the altar. Billy and I were front and center, about two feet from Mrs. Ivers. We got through "Away in the Manger" without a hitch, all the words, everything.

Well, not everything. Billy and I didn't know it, but apparently we couldn't carry a tune in the proverbial basket. So before the choir broke into "O, Little Town of Bethlehem," Mrs. Ivers smiled at Billy and me beatifically and whispered, "Billy, David, this time just move your lips."

And thus ended the singing career of yours truly and his cousin, who moved to California a few months later and never sang again.

After the concert we kids lined up to get our Christmas candy from Santa, whose voice sounded a good deal like Billy's uncle Gustav Steig, the local Lutheran Brotherhood agent. Santa's index finger looked a lot like Gus's also, the finger with which Gus stirred the cream into his coffee whenever he visited our house. Each bag contained unsalted peanuts in the shell, multi-colored ribbon candy, a Delicious apple, one or two "haystacks" (bitter chocolate covering ultra sweet nougat), and little round logs of hard candy with the image of a Christmas tree running through each (How do they do that?).

On the way home, as we tramped through the snow that looked like Lux flakes, Aunt Alma, the gentlest of women, said "Bill, David, what did Mrs. Ivers say to you after the first carol?"

"Oh, nothing much," said Billy, "Just that we sounded great." Billy was an army brat and knew how to operate. I just kept my mouth shut. For the rest of my life.

BILLY BILKS BUCOLICS

Cousin Billy taught us kids on Scranton Street a lot about life. He'd moved around the country, following his father, before Pearl Harbor, and he had big ideas. We learned about that during Christmas vacation, 1945, when it was so cold out that Grandma and Aunt Alma declared skiing and sliding on the Allen Hill off-limits. So the whole gang repaired one morning to the huge old house two doors from ours to play Monopoly, which was the game of choice for kids before the advent of hip-hop, Trivial Pursuit, and Play Station video games.

Our host was Mick Johnson, his Grandma Solsrud, and his mother, church organist Louise Johnson. Seated around the Monopoly board, all of us fortified with Welch's grape juice thoughtfully cut with tap water by Grandma Solsrud, the fight began.

"...No, I get it! I had that stupid tower last time!"

"Then let's shake for it."

"Aah, keep it if you want it so godda. . . ."

"Shh!" whispered Bergie. "Mick's gramma is RELIGIOUS. Ma told me."

"I'll be banker," said Billy, as he grabbed the box and began doling out a rainbow of currency. "Here's ten $100s for you and twenty $50s. . . . and six. . . ."

"What in hel . . . What are ya tryin' to do, Billy? We're only s'pose to get $1500 in all!" Worm Olson was a stickler for rules.

"In Billings, Montana," Billy explained, "we always gave out $3000 right off the bat—made the game last longer."

To that irrefutable logic provided by my city cousin, the gang acquiesced, greedily. And then we shook to see who went first.

"Oh, God . . . gosh . . . Vermont! That's not worth a damn . . . darn. Why cunnit I a got to St. Charles," said rough-talking Chuck Peterson, railing at his fate as if he'd stuck the family fortune in egg futures just before Ancel Keyes discovered cholesterol.

"Woodie, trade you my Connecticut and Baltic for your Pennsylvania. Goebbels [named after Germany's propaganda minister] has already got the other greens and enough money to buy six huses."

"But I've got the other purple and the light blues. I've got two."

"Do it ya dumb farmer, and you'll be sorry."

I did it.

The die, as it were, was cast. My fate was sealed. No Wharton School of Finance for me. Perhaps an English major at Eau Claire State Teacher's College would be best. Round and round we went. Conglomerates were formed, fortunes were made and lost. Clarice Bautch left in a huff at 11:30, her four RRs and both utilities mortgaged, with only two anemic white $1s tucked under her corner of the board. "I'll get my sister to beat up on you guys," she shouted as she stalked out. Billy shuddered, remembering Jackie Bautch, the Polish Amazon, who just last week had taken him by the ankles and inserted him, head first, in a snowpile next to Lovelien's house.

I hung on 'til noon and feasted on Grandma Solsrud's offer of Skippy peanut butter and Nabisco grahams. What the heck? I had one house on Baltic, two on Mediterranean. I was solvent, the West Side's first slumlord.

Then all hell broke loose. Bill landed on Boardwalk, bought it and claimed the last monopoly, "Give me four hotels."

"FOUR? You can't put two hotels on one property!" Worm, the stickler for rules.

"In Billings, Montana, we always did. It ends the game quicker. Besides, what're you guys bitching about? I gave you twice as much money as you were s'pose to have when the game started."

Silence. The moment of truth. Mephistopheles come to claim the collective soul of the guys from Scranton Street. Within minutes, two of us landed on Boardwalk after four hours of missing it like clockwork. Bill broke us, the bank, and everything in sight. Wiping up a fleck of Skippy quivering on Ventnor Avenue, Billy popped the peanut butter into his mug and turned to Mick, our host:

"Got any comic books to trade? I'll give you two old Batmans for that new Wonderwoman—the one where the cover shows her with really pointy you-know-whats."

Silently, the gang stood up, filed out of Grandma Solsrud's, headed for home and five more days until Christmas Eve.

A BUNCH OF FOOLS GO CHRISTMAS FOOLING

My hometown, Whitehall, is only 5 miles from Independence, Wisconsin, but in some respects it might as well be as far away as the moon. When my father was growing up in the 1920s, Whitehall was primarily a Norwegian Lutheran town; Independence was Polish and Roman Catholic. For a time in high school, he dated a Polish girl from Independence. "I'd park my dad's Nash on Hwy. 121 and meet in the cornfield between Mary's farm and the road. Then we'd go to the dance at Midway Pavilion," he recalled.

"Why meet her in the cornfield, Pa?"

"Because if I'd have gone up to the house, her father would have shot me."

So dating across the theological spectrum was a no-no. Even when a Swede married a Norwegian it was considered a "mixed marriage." That's all changed now, and when I go home to see a nephew or niece or friend married, ofttimes the Lutheran pastor and the Catholic priest both function at the ceremony. This a Good Thing.

But when it comes to other customs, the towns remain far apart. When my sister Kip married and moved to Independence, new friends there told her they had heard that she was "a Woodson from home," meaning that her maiden name was Woodson. "No just Wood," replied Kip, to which her Polish neighbors would glance quizzically. We finally figured out that the folks from Independence thought that because of Whitehall's preponderance of Scandinavians everyone's name ended in "son"—Johnson, Olson, Peterson, Woodson.

Back to my story.

When I was growing up, Whitehall people loved to go "Jule Bokking" in the days after Christmas. That's Norwegian for

"Christmas Fooling." It was a family affair, parents dragging high school age kids along for the fun. Here's how it worked. One family—let's call them the Wood family—would get dressed up in costumes and masks. Nothing fancy, you understand, unless you had a theatrical bent or a mother who liked to sew. The younger Wood boy normally dressed up in an old bedsheet with holes cut for eyes. His father, who was theatrical, probably wore a dress and a dustmop wig. After supper, they'd pile into the '50 Pontiac and head for the home of someone they didn't know too well. They'd knock on the door and the host would say, "Clara, there's Jule Bokkers here!" He'd invite them in and they would perform. The father would usually sing "Three Little Fishies" (who "fam and fam all over the dam"). Then the hosts would try to guess who the performers were. That done, Clara would serve a glass of Mogen David and a fattigmand bakkel, a delicacy that recalls a diamond shaped slab of cardboard dipped in powdered sugar.

At that point, the hosts would put on a mask and a makeshift costume and join the Wood family and off they'd all go to their next destination. This would continue through the night—and morning. The last time the Wood family Jule Bokked, they ended up helping a farmer and his wife do the morning milking out in Fuller Coulee. That's a lot of Mogen David.

Jule Bokking died out for a time, until the Ethnic Revival mentioned earlier. But in 1973, a bunch of us ethnicians got together at Betty and Aubyn Smith's Hotel Tap in Independence and decided to try our hand at bringing the old custom back. The wind whipped around the corner of the old hotel while a bunch of us, expatriates from Whitehall, plotted to do some fancy Christmas fooling on the following evening right there in Little Warsaw, where all the taverns have a fancy sign that says "Niema Schlitza, Niema Piwo," which translated means "When you're out of Schlitz, you're out of beer."

What were we thinking of? I don't recall, but probably another round of Schlitz.

We met the next evening at the hotel. Vi Woychik, nee Larson, wore a very authentic looking astronaut costume. My beautiful wife, dressed in Gypsy regalia, looked like she got off the plane from Budapest; Aubyn, taking cue from my father years back, came in drag. Everett Sobotta, the only Polish participant, also came as a woman, a woman with very bushy eyebrows.

First stop: Attorney Ed Kulig's big, beautiful old house on Bugle Lake. R-I-I-I-N-G! Lawyer Kulig came to the door and wondered what was up. We walked right past him and began singing "Kann du glenna gammel Norge?" a famous song composed in Minneapolis that asked the sentimental question, "Can you remember old Norway?"

"How about a drink?" asked Vi.

"Well certainly," said Mrs. Kulig, who had come in from the kitchen. She served us highballs. The Kuligs stared at us for fifteen minutes, as Everett danced a jig. What's up, wondered Lawyer Kulig. What's up, wondered his wife.

We tried two other houses in Independence with the same result. Hmm. And only five miles from Whitehall.

So let's drive there. We did, but with much the same result. We stopped for a libation at Rip's and Jake's Tavern, and a Norwegian-American of our acquaintance said to Everett Sobotta, "Are you Clara Swenson, then?" Clara, a very tall woman with black eyebrows, was the town barber's mother. She had been dead for 20 years. Aubyn hoisted his skirt and used the women's room, and we all went home. So much for an ethnic revival.

But wait! I wrote about our experiences Jule Bokking for the editorial page of the Minneapolis Tribune. Two years later, I received a letter from a man in Brooklyn Center:

"Dear Dave:

"Your story about Jule Bokking in Wisconsin brought back memories from my childhood. So last year I organized our card club and we went around the neighborhood. It was so popular that this year we rented a school bus and went further afield.

"Sincerely, P. Johnson."

What we need in this country are more P. Johnsons. The 1999 Minneapolis phone book lists only 305 of them.

YES, DAVEY, THERE IS A SANTA CLAUS

When Ruth and I arrived in Minneapolis in 1969, we immediately began a Christmas tradition that lasted as long as our favorite restaurants lasted, which wasn't very long. Our faves were Charlie's Café Exceptionale and Harry's, mentioned earlier. Our routine was to eat a lavish luncheon at one of these places and then go shopping downtown, tromping up and down the Nicollet Mall before the Skyway Age took all the glamor— and discomfort—out of wintertime gift-buying. In 1969, I was new at little Augsburg College and feeling my oats with a new Ph.D. That year, we lunched at Charlie's and then headed for Dayton's, now named, for reasons only an overpaid executive could understand, Marshall Field's.

Maybe it was the wine, or maybe the ale in the ale stew I dined on, but I was especially frisky that wintry day. And so when we got into Dayton's, I suggested we go up and see Santa with the other kids (I was 33). Up we went. Without the slightest bit of sheepishness, I stood in line with the real kids. (I thought alcohol was supposed to burn off when used in cooking.) Anyway, I got up to Santa Claus, who was ho-ho-ho-ing with great gusto. Finally, it was my turn. Santa extended a knee for me to sit on, and like an idiot I obliged. He asked me what I'd like for Christmas and I told him—perhaps a Gilbert Chemistry set, a pair of skis with spring bindings, a new Boy Scout uniform.

Santa's response? "We'll see what we can do, Dr. Wood."

"DR. WOOD"!?

Oh-oh. Of all the Santas to pick from in the Twin Cities, I'd picked an Augsburg student. And worse, one who knew me. When school resumed, I slunk around campus for weeks, waiting for the Dean to call me in for irrational behavior. Fortunately for me, the Santa who offered me his knee didn't also offer it to my groin. He must never have told a soul because the students at the insular little campus would have hopped on the story like dogs on a gut cart.

And that's not the end of my affair with Dayton's Santa. Fifteen years later, I had left Augsburg to work as a feature writer at the Star Tribune. One Christmas, my wonderful boss, Hal Quarfoth, God bless him, said he'd just come up with an idea. Why didn't I run down to Dayton's and play Santa for one shift, then write about it for a feature section called "Neighbors"?

"Gee, they're awful persnickety. I'll bet they wouldn't let me do it."

"It's already arranged," said the genial Quarfoth.

The next four hours seemed like a week. I made my way to Santa's locker room, where they togged me out in a Santa costume that weighed about a ton. I began to perspire almost immediately, even before they glued on the fake beard. Then I got my instructions. "NEVER," said the supervisor, "tell a child that you're going to bring him the specific present of his request. Just say Ho-ho-ho a lot and be as evasive as possible." Out I went to face a line of little children that stretched off into the middle distance. After two hours, they called me out for a fifteen-minute break, and I slugged down an icy Coke as fast as if I'd been on a thresher's crew in 100 degree heat. Then back at it for the last half of my shift. "Ho-ho-ho! A Gilbert Chemistry Set, eh? Well, we'll see. Ho-ho-ho!"

My colleague Darlene Pfister dropped by with her camera. She laughed quite a bit to see me suffering in my red togs. Then she took a picture of me being kindly. And soon it was all over. It was the hardest work I ever did for the newspaper, harder even than the day I spent working with a garbage hauler in Edina, after the city editor figured it might be interesting to know what sorts of garbage we'd find in an upscale suburb. (Same old, same old. No patè de fois gras tins, just Grainbelt empties and VanCamp's Pork and Beans cans.)

And so when you see your next Dayton's, er, Marshall Field's Santa, say a little prayer and shoot him a knowing smile.

TWELFTH NIGHT AT THE ANDERSONS

When we lived in south Minneapolis, we had the good fortune to fill our gas tanks and have our old heaps repaired at Kirk's Mobil Station on 46th St. Owner Kirkland Anderson, his wife Alice, and son Kirk, Jr., were always on hand to help, to laugh, and to trade stories with the neighbors who dropped in almost every day to tell stories, short and tall. Inevitably, we became friends.

The Anderson family was black and we were white, but that never seemed to matter. At one point, I wrote a story for the Star Tribune about the oldtimers who hung out at Kirk's station. When I interviewed Kirk, he admitted that he felt more comfortable in his home state of Mississippi than he did in Minneapolis, where he has lived for half a century.

"Really? I asked.

"Really," he replied. "At least down there I know where I stand.

Up here, well. . . ."

The Anderson family stood very well with us, in fact head and shoulders above.

Alice, a registered nurse and effective community activist, doubled as a cashier when things got busy at the station. As if that weren't enough, she was a very loving mother, always thinking about her kids. Forty years ago, when Kirk was just getting the Mobil station going, Alice cast about for a way to wind down after Christmas Day. "We had all sorts of goodies left from the big day, Alice recalled. "The tree was still up. So on the twelfth day after Christmas, I cooked a big pot of chowder for Kirk and the kids. Then we gave everyone their last gift, we took the decorations off the tree and took it outside."

In 1978, she was reading The Link, a wonderful south Minneapolis neighborhood newspaper, which had a story about inviting the neighbors in for Twelfth Night and asking them to bring along some seafood to throw in a pot. "We invited about forty friends and neighbors and they all came. Since then the party has grown to 50 and 60 on some years. Once in awhile, I decide not to do it again. Neighbors call and say 'Alice, are you going to do it this year?' I say maybe not. They say, 'But we'll help you, Alice!' And so I do it again."

Once we became friends, Alice invited Ruth and me. Her guest list was always colorblind, and everyone had a great time. We'd stomp the snow off our boots, while Kirk greeted us and mixed drinks. Alice was always in the kitchen with her daughters cooking up a basic gumbo. Each guest brought a bag of fresh seafood—shrimp, scallops, lobster, oysters, crablegs, clams. These bags we duly dumped into Alice's bubbling caldron. Fragrant aromas filled the room. What a great holiday idea!

When the seafood was cooked, we lined up for a bowl of gumbo, a hunk of French bread, and Alice's excellent tossed salad. Then came dessert.

This was fun, too, for the Andersons always ordered an elaborate bouche de noel from New Orleans. Each person got a piece of the cake. The person who discovered a porcelain replica of the baby Jesus in his or her piece would get a big round of applause. That's because he or she had to pick up the tab for next year's expensive cake. Then gifts were passed out, the tree taken down.

The Anderson party made a perfect closure to the Christmas season. Remember? We started with fish at the church supper after Thanksgiving? And now we've ended the season with more fish after Christmas.

Alice warns readers that it will taste different every year, depending on what the guests decide to bring in their bags. She said that lots of folks tend to bring shrimp, so she uses something different for her basic sauce. Here's a basic gumbo recipe that makes enough for ten people:

> Melt in a skillet 2 tbsp. butter. Add shrimp shells, lobster shells, crab leg leavings that you've saved in the freezer. Saute. Add 3 quarts of water. Simmer covered for two hours. Then add ¼ cup of chopped celery, ¼ cup chopped parsley, ¼ cup chopped onions, ½ tsp. salt, 1 tsp. paprika. Simmer. Strain and retain stock. Saute in 2 tbsp. butter ½ cup chopped onion, ½ cup sliced frozen okra, ½ cup chopped celery with leaves. Add 2 ½ cups chopped tomatoes, 2 tbsp. tapioca, all the soup stock. Simmer for one hour.

And wait for your guests to arrive with bags of seafood.

CHAPTER SEVEN

BETTER TO GIVE, BUT NICE TO RECEIVE

The manner of giving is worth more than the gift.
—Pierre Corneille

As mentioned earlier, my Grandpa and my great uncles, back in the 1870s, were the first Wood kids in recorded history to receive gifts. But that's just the beginning. The presents after the diphtheria epidemic were generous and elaborate, but since then the opulence of the family gifts has teetered back and forth, depending on the family finances, the mood of the nation, the era in which they were given. When I was a little boy, gifts tended to be very modest as the family huddled in the aftermath of The Great Depression. It wasn't always that way. The story goes that when my older cousin Nancy was born, the first grandkid of Grandma and Grandpa, Christmas Eve was an orgy of giving for the little girl. My father recalled that "she sat on the parlor floor, covered in torn wrapping paper with ribbons hanging off her ears, gifts scattered all over the room. When she finished she said 'Is that ALL?'"

But as I look back, it strikes me that there's little correlation between the cost of the gift and the meaning it holds for its recipients. These days, folks find all manner of expensive gifts under the tree—diamonds as big as the Ritz, laptops, trips to

Europe and the Caribbean. Many are taken for granted and soon forgotten. Other gifts stay with the recipient for a lifetime and then some. I'm a book reviewer by occupation, so I own a very substantial personal library of great fiction, history, and biography. But what are my favorite book possessions?

They reside not in my big downstairs library, but up in the bedroom in an antique lawyer's bookcase. This case holds the books that family members gave to other family members at Christmas over the past century. Most of them were given to my grandpa Ralph, who was a constant reader until those dad-blamed cataracts overtook him.

When he was a kid, he received all manner of exciting books, including an anti-tsarist novel, "For Name and Fame: A Tale of the Afghan War," by G. A. Henty, a gift from his stepsister, Bessie, as well as "A Man for the Ages," a biography of Abe Lincoln, by Irving Batcheller.

These titles do not suggest that what he received for Christmas from his parents and his older brothers was Great Literature. One of my favorites is "Battleship Boys on Foreign Service," in which two American boys somehow get into the U.S. Navy at age 14 and are assigned by the Secretary of War to crack a spy ring in France. The battleship boys could give lessons to President George W. Bush in the matter of denigrating the effete French.

Certainly not great literature, but I have read them nonetheless. I read them to try to understand my grandpa's formative years. When I lived with him, and later when I'd sit with him in the big, now-fashionable Adirondack chairs on the front lawn, he struck me as a gentle, principled man, incredibly naïve and trusting. As I reread these yellowed old books about luck and pluck (the title of one of Horatio Alger's most popular fictions), I knew that these gifts from years gone by had inspired him to act like a gentleman, despite what changed in the world around him.

For years I was a bit shamed at my enthusiasm for such "bad" literature. Then I read New Yorker columnist Calvin Trillin's book about his father, a Jewish immigrant from Russia, who became a modestly successful grocer in Kansas City. Trillin tells us that when it was time for him to apply for college, he wanted to attend the University of Missouri and major in journalism, but his father insisted that he go to fancy-schmancy Yale in the Ivy League. The old man moved heaven and earth to get his son admitted, no easy task. Yale has no journalism department (it's too fancy a place to turn out ink-stained wretches like us), so Trillin had to major in English. Of course, when he graduated, his fancy degree opened doors for him that Missouri never would have, and he ended up as a reporter for Time Magazine, went on to the New Yorker, etc., etc.

Trillin always wondered why the old man, who never went to any school, came up with a place like Yale. Years later, Trillin discovered in his father's modest library a set of children's books, the "Dink Stover at Yale" series, which in successive and inspirational volumes told of the daring feats on the field and in the classroom performed by young Stover. He asked his father why in the world he had such books, and the old man replied that he had used the simple little books to learn English when he was studying for his citizenship tests.

One book I especially treasure fell into my hands when my Aunt Doris died. Among her possessions was a book my Grandma Back gave to my mother when she was a little girl, circa 1920. It's a clothbound book with a four-color cover. "Jed the Poorhouse Boy" was written by that most successful of sappy writers, Horatio Alger. It concludes pretty much like all of the Alger books given to my grandfather, my father, my mother: "Not the least gratifying circumstance in his sudden change of fortune was Jed's discovery of a mother—a gracious and beautiful woman—to whom he was drawn in almost instinctive affection. . . ."

That same Aunt Doris always gave me books when I was a grade schooler. They were bound in hardcover, but none cost more than 50 cents. I'm quite certain she purchased them at the dime store in Black River Falls. Some are classics, like the works of Rudyard Kipling or Mark Twain; others reflect the popular culture of the our age: "Gene Autry and the Thief River Outlaws," by Bob Hamilton; "Bonita Granville and the Mystery of Star Island," by Kathryn Heisenfelt. (I was excited about the latter because Bonita Granville starred in a movie I had just seen, "Hitler's Children.") Some are totally inappropriate as gifts for a pre-teen. Aunt Doris was manic-depressive and occasionally lacked good judgment. When I was in sixth grade she gave me a novel, "The G-String Murders," written by burlesque queen Gypsy Rose Lee. It's my favorite of all Aunt Doris's gifts, because it reminds me of her keen sense of humor despite her mental sufferings, and the fact that even at her most manic, she never forgot about her little fat nephew.

To this day, Ruth, an English teacher, and I exchange books at Christmas, even though our occupations dictate that our house will be overfull of them. Just recently, I used a re-issue of Craig Claiborne's "New York Times Cookbook" that Ruth gave me five years ago. I had worn my original copy to shreds. But somehow I had missed the inscription she had written until I took it down to answer a culinary question a few days ago. Here's what she wrote: "Christmas 1998—Here's hoping we wear out another one together. Love, Ruth."

Isn't that sweet?

One of my earliest memories of Christmas came when we lived in Eau Claire, in 1940. I came down with chickenpox just before Christmas. So I was stuck at home with a red quarantine sign on the little apartment house at the foot of Plank Hill. It was a tough blow for a four-year-old. My parents were still recovering from The Great Depression, and Christmas up to that point and for years to come lacked the frills we take for granted today.

So it came as something of a surprise on Christmas Eve when Santa Claus knocked on the door with a great big gift for yours truly. He lumbered to the living room in full regalia with an awkwardly wrapped package, saying "Ho-ho-ho" or some such expression. I ripped and tore the tissue paper to discover a shiny new tricycle, maroon with cream trim. Wow!

"Ho-ho-ho," said Santa, who bent down and gave me a big hug.

"You're not Santa. You're Uncle Floyd," I said petulantly.

I was right. The smell of Harvester cigar residue and maybe two or three Manhattan cocktails with cherry juice hung heavily in the air. Uncle Floyd Amundson was a big shot at Gillette Rubber Company and had done his best to provide me with a merry Christmas, only to be foiled by aroma. I managed to forgive him, and to this day I treasure the memory of that rough-hewn but gentle giant.

Over the years, the presents kept coming, and what they were was never as important as what they meant in my memory.

For example, we moved from Eau Claire back home to Trempealeau County, where my father became a share cropper during World War II. We moved to a big farm near Blair after a hopeless situation on a smaller one, so I left a country schoolhouse with eight grades for a town school that had only two classes in each room, for me third and fourth grade. Miss Margaret Larson was my teacher. She had been my father's teacher a quarter of a century earlier. He warned me that she was stern—something to do with her old maidenhood—but very good. "Work hard for her," he admonished, "and you'll learn something."

Christmas rolled around and classmates drew names and were asked to buy a present that cost no more than 25 cents. Lyman Ericksmoen got my gift, three Classic Comic books. I got really lucky and received the present Gene Toraason brought. Gene was the dentist's son and was used to dealing with real money. My gift? A printing set. A wooden platen, movable rubber type, a pad and ink, which must have cost at least four bits. Pretty nice, and although I didn't know it, the gift was a precursor to my future occupation, journalism.

Then Miss Margaret Larson gave all forty of us a gift. We all got ten lead pencils, yellow, with our names embossed on each in gold. "David Wood" said mine. Talk about cool. I husbanded them for years, grinding them down to the final "Dav" before they hit the wastebasket. My father was right. Miss Margaret Larson was an excellent teacher and later a good friend. When I got my practice teaching assignment as a college senior, she found out I didn't have a car and called to ask if I would like to ride with her back and forth to Blair each day. I got to know a good deal about Miss Margaret Larson on those rides: her disappointments, her little victories, her aspirations, and her old maidenhood. Finally, I told her one day how generous it was for a single woman, the sole support of her aged mother, to give us those pencils years ago. I asked her how much they cost her per pupil.

"About a quarter," she replied sternly, "if you bought them in bulk."

My mother died two months after I got Miss Margaret Larson's special pencils, and I moved to Whitehall to live with my Grandma and Grandpa Wood. They lived in a beautiful old home near the country club but had lost almost everything else in 1929. They eked out a living renting out rooms to bachelors, but now there was a bedroom—mine—that didn't gross them $3 per week. So Christmases were pretty lean.

I well remember the Christmas vacation when I was in fourth grade. An icy wind whistled down the wastes of Scranton Street on December 26, but that didn't keep Worm Olson, Bergie, Mick Johnson, Gale "Goebbels" Gabriel, Chuck

Peterson, and me from struggling into our mackinaws and trudging out to find out what the other kids found under the Christmas tree.

Bergie was very happy with his new pair of skis, seven-foot pointy pine affairs with SPRING bindings, way better than slices of rubber inner tube that most kids used.

"I got seven-footers, too, with spring bindings AND ski boots," said Chuck Peterson. (He was the kid who had so many toy automobiles that he'd Scotch-tape 3 inch firecrackers to them, roll them down Berg's slanting driveway and laugh when they blew to smithereens.)

Mick Johnson got a Monopoly set with metal movers. Way better than wooden ones.

"I got Monopoly, too, and Parcheesi and Rook and Chinese Checkers." Peterson again.

Worm gloated over his new basic Erector set.

"I got the BIG Erector set with an electric motor and flexible coupling, and also the biggest tube of TinkerToys." Peterson.

"Goebbels" (the war had ended, but his nickname went on) got a Gilbert chemistry set with 24 vials of chemicals.

"I got the one with 48 vials." Guess who?

"Whadja get, Woodie?" the others chorused.

I hung back, wiping snot with a crisp woolen sleeve and kicking the hard snow with my four-buckle overshoe.

"Oh, I got lots."

"C'mon, Woodie! Whadja get?"

"Ah . . . I got a bedspread."

"You gotta be kidding!"

"Well, Grandma said I needed one real bad, so that's what I got."

"You gotta be kidding!"

"It's light blue and it's got P-40 fighter planes embroidered into it," I said and drifted down the street toward home.

Grandpa came and sat down by me on the mohair couch in the parlor, put his giant hands on his knobby knees. "What's wrong, Davey? Why aren't you out with the other kids?"

"Oh, I don't know. I was cold, I guess."

A trace of tear began to come.

"Didn't you like Christmas?" asked the old man, as he opened his pen knife and carved off a tiny sliver of rock-hard Piper Heidsieck plug tobacco and slid it into his lower lip. He never spit.

"Christmas was . . . great."

"Didn't you like your present? It was about all we could afford this year. Maybe next . . ."

My tear trace became a torrent.

"Davey, I have something you might like. Come on into the kitchen."

Grandpa put a gnarly paw to the cupboard door, opened it, dug around in a coffee can and came out with a pocket watch. It had a winder an inch long, and on its face, which was the size of a small pancake, there was a word: WESTCLOX.

"I don't use it any more, so it's yours," said Grandpa.

I stuffed it into my overall pocket, put on my mackinaw and raced out the door to rejoin the guys.

In the years to come, the Wood family fortunes improved. I got hickory skis in seventh grade, a full-bore Boy Scout Uniform in eighth (I hadn't the heart to tell my father I'd quit the BSA). I got my Gilbert chemistry set and once a miniature pool table, the cardboard bed of which sagged a bit. The Christmas before high school graduation I got an expensive wristwatch. But looking back, Grandpa's pocket watch was the best gift I ever got.

A framed tintype of my grandpa as a little boy, makes a great Christmas tree ornament.

So does a varnished lobster shell

Our family saves everything, including greeting cards sent to great uncle Jim, the dipftheria survivor, and his wife Ollie.

Here's Dave, sweating it out at Dayton"s with a banjo—no, that's a kid—on his knee.

Ruth's and Dave's first Christmas party, Cedar Avenue, Minneapolis, 1969. I'm the skinny guy on the left; Ruth is the one with the knees at center. The tree cost two bucks.

The neighbor girls, Tina and Anna Keane, and their mother Effie put the finishing touches on a grapefruit half stabbed with shrimp on toothpicks

Anna Crandall of the Little Wagon, a fabled Star Tribune hangout, always helped out at our Christmas parties. Dave stands behind to "supervise."

Literary treasures from a bygone era. Will Rebecca of Sunnybrook farm ever meet that cute Battleship Boy?

Grandpa Ralph got a piggy bank for Christmas about a century ago. Or is that called a horsy bank? He never saved any money and neither did I.

A holiday feast winds down. Dick and Sue Beckham, Jon and Gretchen Hassler listen to someone's wisdom. Is that guy smoking? Is this Minnesota?

Leftovers anyone? One year we invited a bunch over for a New Year's Eve party to eat up the Christmas goodies. Dick Caldwell's and my tuxedos were the stalest items served up.

A wedding anniversary for Grandma and Grandpa Wood. He was partial to "hot ones," she to chow mein. After fifty years of ingesting both, they were still alive and kicking.

Dave and Ruth Wood eating someone else's food.

Aunt Irene Pirsig gave us one of the three kings—we don't know which—to top our tree. It ranks right up there with the Tuffy and the lobster shell as decorations go.

Greavlax! M-m-m, good!!

Dave, as Santa, cuddles up to a Dayton's customer.

We always had help from friends. Coral Samson and Grace Sulerud help butter lefse, Norway's answer to Lebanese Pita, Mexican tortillas, Armenian lavosh and just about every other flatbread in the world.

Ingebretsen's Market on Lake Street in "Summertime, when the lutefiskin' is easy...." with apologies to "Porgy and Bess."

Else Pirsig in Oak Lawn, Illinois, sitting by a Christmas tree from her Post-Tuffy era.

Family and friends partake of oyster stew and rollepolse sandwiches on Christmas Eve.

One year the German side of the family invaded our home at Christmas. The guy sitting under the Virgin Mary is Uncle Clarence Schwarz, who contributed the pfefferneuse recipe for this book. The lady in red and white is Elsie Pirsig, the popcorn ball lady.

CHAPTER VIII

WE DINE ON CHRISTMAS EVE

Oh Lord support us all the day long,
until the shadows lengthen and the evening comes,
and the busy world is hushed,
and the fever of life is over, and our work is done.
—Cardinal Newman

A BREAD FOR ALL THE CHRISTMAS SEASON

Before we get down to business on the Christmas Eve meal, here's a recipe for a wonderful bread you can use throughout the year, but most especially at Christmas.

A few weeks before the parade of Christmas dining, I make a big batch of light rye bread that's good enough to swim the Vistula river for. I use it in various permutations, for hors d'ouevres, for toast before church on Christmas morning. It doesn't look like much. There's so little rye flour in it that it looks like plain white bread. But its density is such that it holds up well under any circumstance. First, however, readers will like to know its background.

It was a sad day in Independence, Wisconsin, when the state inspectors blew in and told the Polish ladies they could no longer bake bread in their ancient outdoor ovens and sell it to townsfolk, like my sister Kip. The old ovens were made of brick and stood in many a farm's backyard. The ladies built wood fires right in the clay oven and when the ashes were just right, they scraped the detritus out and—horrors!—tossed naked loaves of bread dough right onto the hot surface, closed the steel oven door and waited for the big round loaves to be done.

Inspectors didn't like what they saw. Sometimes the finished loaves had flecks of ash on them. It didn't matter that their husbands—Stanislaus, Roman, Ignatz, and Leo—and lots of neighbors had wolfed down huge slabs of the stuff for the past century, this had to stop. And so it stopped, and my sister had serious light rye withdrawal symptoms, as well as hallucinations, until she persuaded her friend Marge Pape, a Polish baker, to share her recipe. Kip and I have been baking the stuff in our kitchen ranges ever since. It's a big recipe, enough to feed the entire corps of Polish lancers on their way to encounter the German Panzer divisions in 1939. But if you wrap it well it freezes nicely. Here's how Marge does it, in her words:

You'll need 3 cups of lukewarm water, 4 cups of lukewarm potato water (I cheat by throwing some instant mashed potato flakes in plain water), 1 Tbsp. plus 1 tsp granular yeast, 2 cups of medium rye flour, 3 heaping Tbsp. of salt, 2 Tbsp. of vegetable oil, 18 cups unbleached white flour.

Mix in a very large pan 3 cups lukewarm water, 1 Tbsp. sugar and yeast. Let stand 20 minutes. Then add 4 cups potato water, 2 cups rye flour and 5 cups white flour. Stir until smooth (a wire whisk works just fine). Let his mixture rise until it drops. Then add oil, 1 cup flour and salt. Mix, slowly adding remaining flour to form a soft ball. A very BIG soft ball. Knead until the dough is no longer sticky, about 10 minutes. Place in a greased bowl and let rise until double in size. Make six loaves of equal size and place in greased bread tins (if you're aiming for Polish authenticity, toss in some crushed charcoal for nostalgia's sake) and poke the tops of each four times with table fork tines. Let rise about 1 hour. Brush with salad or olive oil. Bake in oven for about 50 minutes. Decant and let cool.

To serve: slice thinly, butter, and layer with Norwegian gravlax for a truly mixed marriage. It's also great toasted.

A MELTING POT CHRISTMAS EVE SUPPER

After my mother's death in 1945, my father remarried in 1948, and lots of things were to change. The bride, Edna Johnson, owned a restaurant on Main Street in Whitehall, and never again did I eat a single-scoop ice cream cone. Edna was a lavish cook. Money spent on food was no object. And so never again did I eat Grandma Wood's Tuesday night special all winter: a soupdish of bacon drippings into which we poured Karo syrup, whipped it into a froth and dipped stale bread heels into.

Since Edna was 100 percent Norwegian, we were initiated into the mysteries of potato dumplings, lots of blood sausage, flaky sandbakkels, krumkake ("diplomas," was what my father called them), sharp-edged and ornate rosettes ("like eating razor blades," my father said), light-as-a-feather lefse, and, of course, lutefisk.

It's not that we hadn't eaten lutefisk before. My grandmother had cured it from scratch, getting the baseball bat-like slabs piled up outside Erickson's store after every loose dog in town had peed on it. She'd soak the hard fish in lye water, then several baths of fresh. I liked it. A lot. And so did my father and Yankee grandpa. But we never ate it on Christmas Eve. That was the night when we ate oyster stew.

But then came our first Christmas Eve with Edna and my new stepbrother, Doug. Before the presents were to be opened the whole tribe gathered for dinner at the house Dad and Edna were renting. The kitchen where the card tables had been shoved together and clothed was hot and steamy. There was a smell of lutefisk in the air and there was something else that wasn't quite smellable. But a rich unctuousness pervaded the room. It wasn't the brandy I smelled on the breath of my well-off uncle, or even his expensive shaving lotion.

Then what was it? The first course, of course. Oyster stew. Oyster stew followed by lutefisk?

That's right. Edna, God bless her, wouldn't eat an oyster if she were trapped with the Starving Armenians. But she wanted her new relatives to feel comfortable, so everyone got a steaming bowl of oyster stew, plump oysters swimming around in a melted butter slick above a heady mixture of half and half. "I hope this is okay," she said. "I'm not used to making it." It was more than okay, although I don't think brother Doug liked it much. My little sister Kip didn't either. She didn't like anything. But I slurped it up fast enough. When Edna noticed I had eaten all my oysters, she ladled hers into my broth, explaining that she could tolerate her broth, but wouldn't eat an oyster if she were trapped with the Starving Armenians.

The stew finished, Edna served up huge platters of lutefisk, expertly poached, not the kind of fillets you can see through. Then came homemade lefse, mashed rutabagas, coleslaw, boiled potatoes, meatballs, and melted butter. It all looked delicious, except to Kip, age 6, who toyed with a lone meatball and kept looking out to the tree in the living room to see if she could spot her presents.

I dug into the slippery stuff and ate a lot. But somehow the chemistry—and I don't mean that metaphorically—wasn't just right. Our new family learned that night an important lesson: oysters and lutefisk do not mix. Perhaps if we had been blessed with cows' multiple stomachs we'd have been hunky-dory. The oysters might have been stored in one stomach, the lutefisk in another. But such was not the case. Each of us had only one stomach, and inside it burbled the bivalves and the stokkefisk and the lye. The well-off uncle was the first to excuse himself. His single stomach was filled with bivalves, stokkefisk, lye and Christian Brothers. He headed for what he thought was the back door and, well, relieved the burbling right into Edna's new pantry.

"I thought that was the back door," he said sheepishly.

"No," said Emil Johnson, Edna's father. "We added on two years ago."

"Oh," said the well-off uncle and to his wife, "Well, I guess we better eat and run."

We got through that evening, tore open the presents, then had desserts: fattigmand bakkels, date-filled cookies, and mocha cake.

When I retired to bed with my new Boy Scout Manual, there was a burning in my being that didn't come from any enthusiasm for camping safety or the proper handling of a tent pole.

After that first Christmas, Christmas Eve was a simpler affair. Normally, we'd have a lighter supper and go to late services at Our Saviour's, where Doug and I were soon bound for confirmation class (but that's another book, a book called Luther's Small Catechism).

What Edna finally settled on for a menu was a fine melting pot supper. Oyster stew from the Yankee side; rollepolse sandwiches from the Scandinavian contingent. I don't know which I like better. So these days here's what Ruth and I and our guests eat before presents and a trip to a midnight service:

Rollepolse Sandwiches
Dill Pickles
Oyster Stew
Oyster Crackers
Salted Mixed Nuts
Ruby Port

Rollepolse Sandwiches

My father ate these excellent meat sandwiches (pronounced
RUE-la-pulse-a) long before he ever met his new Scandinavian
bride. In fact, he always said he looked forward to the death of
members of the Swedish side of the family up in Hale Township
because it meant there'd be rollepolse sandwiches after the
funeral at Elk Creek church. I think he was only partly kidding.

> 1 flank steak (any size because this stuff keeps for a long
>   time)
> ½ finely minced onion
> Kosher salt and cracked pepper to taste
> Poultry seasoning to taste
> Water to cover
> 2 bay leaves
> A few allspice berries
> Needle and thread
> Butcher string
> Bread pan
> Brick

Lay flank steak on its visceral side, with the open striated flesh
facing you. Trim bits off the edges so your steak is a rectangle.
Finely chop the trim. Cut shallow slashes into striated flank.
Sprinkle with salt, pepper, and poultry seasoning. Distribute
evenly minced onion and chopped trim onto the slashed meat
and roll tightly, into a summer sausage. Sew it up along the
loose edge from stem to stern. It will look slightly lopsided.

Now take lengths of butcher string and tie the sausage tightly about every 1 inch. Place in heavy kettle with water to cover, plus bay leaves, allspice. Simmer slowly until tender (perhaps 2 hours). Remove from kettle, place in plastic bag, place in high-sided bread pan lengthwise, place brick on top of meat and refrigerate for at least two days. The heavier the weight, the better the outcome. When it's adequately pressed, cut off butcher string, pull out thread, and slice thinly. Place on buttered slices of thinly sliced Polish Light Rye (see recipe above).

Oyster Stew

Everyone has a favorite recipe for oyster stew. One of the best I ever ate was at Durgin Park, near Fanieul Hall, in Boston. There, the chef shucked the select oysters fresh and just out of the ocean, sauteed them in a steamer in gobs of butter, added half & half and whipping cream. That last was a bit much and if anything, my recipe is less rich than most I've read about.

> (4 generous servings)
> 2 ounces butter
> ¼ cup finely minced onions (optional)
> 1 pound shucked oysters, drained and liquid reserved
> 3 cups whole milk
> 1 cup half and half
> Kosher salt and cracked pepper
> Premium brand oyster crackers

Melt butter in heavy kettle. Cook onions translucent. Add drained oysters and saute until edges begin to curl. Add milk and cream. Simmer and add as much oyster liquid as your tastebuds can handle (usually all of it). Season with salt and pepper and serve with oyster crackers. No other shape or texture will do!

When my uncle Charlie Briggs, longtime milk hauler, came to dinner for oyster stew, he'd eat about five bowls and then stretch out behind the wood-burning cookstove and sleep until Aunt Hazel woke him and told him it was time to go home. I usually try to hold myself to one open faced rollepolse sandwich and one serving of stew. Then we retreat to the tree for presents, the ruby port to sip, the nuts to nibble on.

This makes for a thoroughly wonderful evening—as long as you remember to attend midnight services at the church of your choice.

CHAPTER IX

A MULTI-ETHNIC CHRISTMAS DINNER

Strange to see how a good dinner and feasting
reconciles Everybody.
—Samuel Pepys

O ur Christmas dinners vary from year to year. Only one thing is constant: we surround ourselves with as many friends and relatives as can make it to River Falls. Here's a sample of a meal we might serve that draws its inspiration from beyond the boundaries of Pierce County, Wisconsin. I have no doubt that this menu will be roundly condemned by the American Medical Association and the entire staffs of the Pierce and St. Croix County Health Departments, as well as the national office of the Women's Christian Temperance Union. But what of it? Christmas comes but once a year, and the AMA and other medical gurus have been wrong before. (Remember how unhealthy eggs used to be?) As for the WCTU, it would be impolite to mention the Prohibition amendment, so I'm not going to tackle them. If alcohol is a problem, physical or otherwise, just leave it out and add a little more cholesterol.

Grandpa Wood's "Hot Ones"
Poland's "Cold Ones"
Gravlax hors d'ouevres on Polish light rye

Ribeye Roast
Yorkshire Pudding
Ruthie's Orange and Onion Salad
Steamed Asparagus
Aunt Wylis's Plum Pudding with Hard Sauce

Grandpa Wood's "Hot Ones"

Until cataracts rendered Grandpa unable to walk uptown to Roy
Fortun's drugstore, his trip was a yearly ritual before each
Christmas. His mission: One pint of 190 proof grain alcohol.
His intent: To concoct a punch to knock the socks off family
members before we sat down to Christmas dinner. I'm certain
his Baptist parents had they known would have been very
disappointed in Grandpa, who stopped going to church when
he reached his majority and never went back until his funeral.
But that didn't stop him from spouting Bible passages learned
as a youth or celebrating Christmas with something very
special. One hundred ninety proof was indeed special. When I
was a kid it was illegal to sell such hooch in a tavern, thus the
trip to Roy Fortun, who charged an arm and a leg for the stuff
that's three times as potent as today's vodka. It's now
available in any Wisconsin liquor store for about ten dollars.
Hot ones were definitely a non-Baptist drink. Grandpa learned
the recipe from his hired man, a Norwegian immigrant who
drank it in great quantities during the winter seasons. (It isn't
the sort of drink to take into the hay mow of a summer day.)

> **For one drink:**
> 1 ounce 190 proof grain alcohol
> 1 small strip of lemon peel
> 1 sugar cube
> 3 ounces boiling water

With a wooden muddler, crush the sugar lump and muddle in
the oil of the lemon peel in a small crystal goblet or wine glass.

Pour in alcohol. Top with boiling water. Drink. (But not more than two!)

Poland's "Cold Ones"

My friend Robert T. Smith was a long-time columnist for the Minneapolis Star Tribune. Long before I knew him, Bob worked as a reporter stationed in Paris for Time Magazine. While there, he hung around with Russian expatriates, oldtimers who got out when the Tsar was overthrown. They taught Bob that the proper accompaniment for anything fishy, from caviar to salmon, was potato vodka, preferably Polish. That's available these days in quality liquor stores. Buy a quart and then prepare a place for it with:

> 1 empty ½ gallon milk carton, thoroughly rinsed
> 1 quart of water and a few drops of food coloring of your
>   choice

Take staple out of milk carton mouth and open the carton fully. Place bottle of vodka in dead center of carton's bottom. Pour colored water to cover largest part of bottle, leaving neck exposed. Place in freezer. When frozen, tear off carton, wrap bottom in a pretty washcloth and pour vodka into tiny chilled goblet. Drink (But not more than two, unless you're Russian.)

Gravlax

Here's Norway's bow to Jewish cuisine. Whenever we're in New York City, Ruth looks forward to Sunday morning when she sends me out into the concrete caverns in search of a delicatessen. I pick up a Sunday edition of the New York Times, hoping I won't need hernia surgery until we get home, and then it's on to the meat counter where I pick up half a pound of lox, or "nova" as they call it in Gotham. Then a carton of cream cheese ("schmear") and finally some giant white bagels. Then it's back to the hotel, where we while away the morning marvelling at the real estate prices and eating bagels and lox until they come out our ears.

Frankly, I prefer the Norwegian version of cured salmon, called gravlax or gravedlax. Legend has it that years ago, Norwegians seasoned a whole salmon (lax) and dug a hole or grave (grav), tossed in the salmon, covered it with dirt and dug it up a year later and ate it on rye bread. I have a more civilized and probably less dangerous recipe for a delicious hors d'ouevre, which I adapted from a recipe in James Beard's fish cookbook.

> 1 ½ lbs. red salmon with skin still on (preferably from the Pacific)
> ¼ lb. kosher salt
> ¼ lb light brown sugar
> 1 bunch fresh dill
> 1-2 oz. unflavored akavit or Polish (this is a melting pot book, right?) vodka
> 2 feet of butcher string
> 1 plastic bag with holes punched in it
> 1 wire rack
> 1 cake pan big enough to hold the wire rack
> 1 full six pack of diet Coke or Leinenkugel's beer

Mix the sugar and salt thoroughly. Rub as much of the mixture into the fleshy seams of the fillet. Chop half the dill finely and sprinkle dill and akavit or vodka on fillet. (Save remaining dill for garnish later.) Cut fillet in two. Put pieces together, skin side out. The fillet will be tapered, so attempt to match the narrow side of one piece with the thick side of the other. Tie firmly with spring. Place in bag with punched holes. Place rack in cake pan. Place bagged salmon on rack. Place six-pack on salmon (a delicate balance!) and put it all in fridge. Leave for at least five days. The six-pack will press out unwanted liquid while the fish cures. Once the curing process is over, untie the packet, rinse the by now dessicated dill off under cold water tap. Dry with paper towels. With a sharp knife, carve fillet across the grain into thin slices.

Now it's time to assemble the hors d'ouevre. Slice as thinly as possible the dense Polish light rye (see recipe above). Trim off crusts and cut each slice in half. Spread with softened butter to which you have added Dijon mustard and chopped dill to taste. (Heavy on the dill and light on the mustard, to my taste.) Put a slice of salmon on each half-slice, garnish with fresh basil leaves or sprigs of dill, put on platter and serve with "Hot Ones" or "Cold Ones." Enjoy!

Most fancy restaurants serve gravlax with a lemony sauce and dark pumpernickel. That's a big mistake, I think, because those flavors intrude on the very delicately flavored salmon, which by now is buttery in texture and irresistible.

Ribeye Roast

Here's our main tribute to my family's English heritage. "Roast Beef and England, England and Roast Beef," goes the first line of an 18th century song attributed to novelist Henry Fielding. On any other day, I'd prefer an overdone pot roast, but on this special day I want my roast to be medium rare. I used to make standing rib roasts, but have found that if you're serving fewer than 10 people, the standing rib doesn't stand tall enough for easy carving. So for years we've been using the more compact ribeye roast, which also takes less time to cook. It is simply a bunch of rib steaks that haven't been sliced. If they're not out on the display section, just ask the butcher to cut a chunk to your specifications.

> 6 ounces meat per serving.
> 1-2 cloves garlic
> Kosher salt
> Cracked pepper
> ½ cup flour
> 1-2 cups canned low-salt beef broth
> 2 Tbsp. prepared horseradish
> ½ cup half & half
> 1 tsp. sugar

Peel garlic and slice thinly. With the sharp point of a knife, insert slivers into meat at a depth of 1 ½ inches. Rub surface of meat with salt, pepper, and finally, flour. Place meat on rack in a 450 degree preheated oven. Cook for 25 minutes and reduce temperature to 300. Every hunk of beef is different, and so is every oven; thus getting your roast to the proper doneness is tricky. Rule of thumb is 18 to 20 minutes per pound for medium rare, 16 to 18 minutes for rare, and 20 to 22 minutes for medium, 26 to 30 for well-done. (Cooks who do the latter to a ribeye should be subject to public service sentences.) But these rules aren't your only option. The best present my darling wife every gave me—besides herself—is a tiny chef's thermometer, which rests in a slender cylindrical holster in my breast pocket. Open the oven door and stick it into the meat for an instantaneous temperature reading. Forewarned is forearmed. Be prepared to serve a bit earlier—or a bit later—than you expect. So have your sauce—a mixture of horseradish, sugar, salt, and half & half—mixed to your taste.

When your thermometer reads just a bit less than your desired doneness, remove roast from rack, cover with foil, and let rest on the counter for at least 20 minutes before slicing. Pour drippings from pan into holding cup. Loosen browned bits on the bottom of the pan with beef broth, add a bay leaf and perhaps a splash of ruby port wine and reduce by half for a thin sauce. Now take the drippings and prepare another English favorite:

Yorkshire Pudding

My ancestors were kicked out of Yorkshire in the late 16th century for refusing to baptize their infant children. It must have been hell for them to leave behind this delicacy.

(12 servings—What's left over, toss out into a snowbank for the birds. They'll love it!)

Have the following ingredients at the ready, but no more than an hour before it goes in the oven. As soon as the roast is out, turn oven temperature to 400.

     1 ¾ cups flour
     1 teaspoon salt
     1 cup milk (room temperature!)
     4 eggs beaten fluffy (room temperature!)
     1 cup water (room temperature!)

Sift flour and salt into a bowl. Make a well in mixture's center. Stir in milk. Add beaten eggs and stir them into the batter. Add water. Beat the batter until bubbles rise to the top. Put beef drippings in two 9x12 pans to a depth of ¼ inch. If drippings are insufficient, add melted butter. (I told you the AMA would disapprove!) When oven reaches 400 degrees, re-beat the batter, pour into pans, and bake the puddings for about 20 minutes. Reduce heat to 350 and bake for another 10 minutes. Remove from oven and cut into squares. Serve at once right out of the pan.

Ruthie's Deerslayer Salad

One of the standing jokes in our family is my father's deer hunting expeditions. For many decades, he and his pals from Whitehall would journey all the way north to Iron River for a week. The older they got, the less they hunted, preferring the night clubs of Iron River, where they danced with retired schoolmarms from Superior, who "just happened to drop by." They also did a good deal of eating. The first time my bride ran into my father after one of his hunting junkets, she asked him how hunting was. "No deer," replied the old man, "But we cooked in the cabin the day before we left. Oscar Lovelien made a wonderful prime rib and served orange and onion salad alongside."

That sounded pretty good to Ruthie, but she never asked Oscar for the recipe, so she made up her own, which does a great job of cutting through all the grease that goes into this rather excessive menu. It also adds a fine splash of color.

(for 8 people)

1/3 cup olive oil
3 Tbsp. orange juice
1 Tbsp. lemon juice
½ tsp. minced rosemary leaves
½ tsp. kosher salt
cracked pepper to taste
6 large oranges, sliced, de-pithed and seeded
1 medium red onion, sliced into rings
8 large leaves of romaine or any leafy lettuce

Mix first six ingredients. Shake until emulsified and pour over orange and onion slices. Marinate for one hour. Arrange lettuce on salad plates, arrange orange slices on lettuce. Garnish with 3 or 4 red onion rings.

Steamed Asparagus

More health and more color with this easy recipe. To my mind, a microwave oven isn't worth the kilowatts to blow it to Hades, unless you need to cook asparagus.

(for 8 people)

40 asparagus spears
2 ounces softened butter
Kosher salt and cracked pepper to taste

Trim asparagus by snapping off bottoms by hand. This will avoid any tough woody ends. Rinse thoroughly. Place across the bottom of a microwaveable pan. Just before serving, splash on half a cup of water. Loosely cover with plastic wrap and microwave for about 90 seconds or until spears are still firm to the bite. Drain, smear with a bit of butter, salt, and pepper and serve.

Aunt Wylis's Plum Pudding

My mother's sister Wylis is one of the world's great cooks. When she married my Uncle Eugene Harlow, she fell in with a family of Scots from Perth. They knew how to cook, as I found out when I went to live with them very briefly just after my mother died. One of my favorite desserts and one especially appropriate to Christmas is plum pudding. It ain't easy, but worth the try.

(24 servings)

1 cup all-purpose flour
1 pound chopped suet (about 2 cups)
1 pound raisins
1 pound dried currants
½ pound chopped citron
1 whole grated nutmeg pod
1 Tbsp. cinnamon
½ Tbsp. mace
1 tsp. salt
½ cup brown sugar
7 egg yolks
7 egg whites whipped stiff
¼ cup cream
½ cup brandy
3 cups grated fresh bread crumbs

Are you ready? Take a bit of the flour and lightly dredge the suet and dried fruit. Mix the spices with the remaining flour. Combine the above with the egg yolks, cream, brandy, and bread crumbs. Fold in the whipped egg whites. Pour this batter into a greased mold and steam slowly for six hours. Top with hard sauce (see below) and have the neighbors in to enjoy dessert. Don't let the steaming put you off. If you don't have a mold, use two-pound coffee cans. Pour the cans or mold only 2/3 full, cover tightly and place them on a rack or trivet in a heavy kettle. Add boiling water until it's halfway up the mold. Cover kettle and put on hot burner. When steam starts to escape, turn down heat to low and six hours later you'll be ready to unmold.

Hard Sauce

This, as it were, is the frosting on the pudding.

(Makes 2 cups. You've got the neighbors coming, right?)

2 cups powdered sugar
10 tbsp. softened butter
¼ tsp. salt
2 tsp. of vanilla (or brandy)
½ cup cream

Gradually beat sugar into softened butter. Add seasonings. When thoroughly mixed, beat in cream. Chill and serve it cold on plum pudding that has reached room temperature.

CHAPTER EIGHT

RECIPES FOR A CHRISTMAS PARTY

1. Aunt Myrt's Breakfast Food of Champions

About fifty Decembers ago, I dropped by my aunt Myrtle Amundson's house near the campus where I attended college. She was finishing up her annual present project. She saved all manner of containers over the year, spray-painted them in gay colors, then filled them with her "breakfast food of champions" and passed them out to friends. She gave me a two pound Hills Brothers Coffee can full, with the warning not to open before Christmas. I left Myrt soon after and ate most of what she called "nuts and bolts" before I reached my hovel.

> ½ cup butter
> 2 tbsps. Worcestershire sauce
> 4 dashes Louisiana hot sauce
> 4 ½ cups Cheerios
> 4 ½ cups bite-size rice chex
> 2 cups bite-size wheat chex
> 2 cups straight pretzel sticks
> 2 cups Spanish peanuts
> 1 ½ tsps. salt
> ½ tsp. garlic powder

Heat oven to 325 degrees. Melt butter in large roasting pan. Add Worcestershire and hot pepper sauces. Stir in dry ingredients. Sprinkle with salt and garlic powder. Toss thoroughly. Bake for about 45 minutes, stirring from time to time. Try not to eat it all before your guests arrive.

2. Marcella Hazan's Sweet and Sour Fish

I'm no friend of Venetian cookbook guru Marcella Hazan. (Don't worry! I hear she's very crabby.) Her cookbooks, however, are great. This sweet and sour number is eminently flexible and always draws compliments.

> 1 lb. sole fillets
> ¼ cup of seedless raisins soaked in water and drained
> flour
> vegetable oil
> 2 tbsp. extra virgin olive oil
> 1 ½ cups of thinly sliced onions
> 1 cup white wine vinegar
> 1 tsp. granulated sugar
> 1 tsp. salt
> 3 tbsp. pine nuts.

Cut fillets into two inch pieces. Coat with flour. Fry in vegetable oil. Pat dry on paper towel and place pieces edge to edge in a shallow casserole dish. Clean fry pan. Saute onions in olive oil, sugar, and salt on low heat in covered pan for about 15 minutes until onions are completely limp but not caramelized. Remove cover, increase heat and cook off any liquid until onions begin to caramelize. Add vinegar, increase heat to high and boil for three to four minutes. Take off heat. Sprinkle fish with raisins and pine nuts. With slotted spoon, take onions out of vinegar and place on fish. Pour vinegar mixture on fish. Cover with plastic wrap and let marinate for at least 12 hours. This traditional Italian recipe makes a great party dish because it is best eaten at room temperature. If you don't care for fish, use an equal amount of thinly sliced pork tenderloin.

3. Mary Hart's Big Easy Cheesy

Years ago I told my Star Tribune colleague Mary Hart, long-time food editor, that we had guests coming and I was unprepared to provide an hors d'ouevre at cocktail hour. She said, "Oh, that's so easy." She gave me this very simple recipe that doesn't sound great, but is one of the big hits of every Christmas party since. Take one 8 ounce package of Philadelphia Cream Cheese. Unwrap while cold. Toast 1/3 cup of sesame seeds in a dry fry pan, stirring frequently until light brown. Let cool. Roll block of cheese in sesame seeds, place in a high-lipped plate to which you've added ¼ inch of soy sauce. Sprinkle chopped fresh chives or green onion tops on cheese. Serve with thin crackers.

4. Dave's Faux Hummus

I call this "false" because the hummus I like best is lacking one key ingredient, which I think tastes something like the sludge at the bottom of an automobile's crank case. Years ago, I sampled the hummus at Emily's Lebanese Delicatessen in northeast Minneapolis. It was delicious, light, and fluffy. I asked why it was different than most hummus you get. The clerk: "Because we don't use sesame paste." Aha! Here's a recipe for a small batch:

> 1 can chickpeas
> ¼ cup olive oil
> 2 cloves of garlic
> salt and white pepper to taste
> fresh mint and pine nuts to garnish

Drain and rinse chickpeas. Simmer in water for five minutes. Drain and cool in ice water. Drain again. Rub lightly to remove as many husks as possible. Process in food processor until finely ground. Add oil, and garlic that you've passed through a press, add salt and pepper. At this stage, you may want to add a bit more oil to make the hummus creamier. Spread on a flat plate, garnish with mint and pine nuts. Serve with warm pita bread cut into triangles.

5. Jane Harred's Cheese Thins

I had a favorite recipe for homemade cheese wafers until I moved to River Falls and ate at our neighbors Jane and Larry Harred's and tasted Jane's version. I'm a convert. Here's a recipe from Jane that will yield about five dozen wafers.

> 1/3 cup wheat germ
> ½ cup butter at room temperature
> 1 cup grated extra sharp cheddar (about 4 ounces)
> ½ tsp. dried mustard
> 1 ½ tsp. salt, divided
> 1/8 to ¼ tsp. cayenne pepper (plus extra for garnish)
> 1 cup all-purpose flour (plus extra for kneading dough)

Heat oven to 350 degrees. Toast wheat germ in shallow baking pan in oven, shaking occasionally, for 8-10 minutes until lightly browned. Watch it like a hawk! Cool. Beat butter in medium bowl until light and fluffy. Stir in cheese, mustard, and cayenne. Stir in flour and wheat germ. Dough will be dry and crumbly, but have heart. Turn it out onto floured work surface and knead until it becomes smooth. Roll into a log about an inch in diameter and 16 inches long. Wrap tightly in plastic and refrigerate for up to a week. To bake: preheat oven to 400 degrees. Lightly butter two baking sheets. Cut dough into slices about ¼ inch thick. Place on prepared baking sheets. Sprinkle lightly with remaining salt, to which you can mix in a bit more cayenne pepper. Bake 8-10 minutes until golden brown. Remove from oven and leave on baking sheets a few minutes before transferring to rack to cool. Store up to 3 days in airtight container.

6. Larry Harred's Green Olive Tapenade

Ruth's colleague in the UW-River Falls English Department taught for a time in Spain and makes the most fantabulous paella I've ever swallowed, but that's another story. He also makes a tapenade that is a knockout at Christmas parties.

> 2 cups pitted green olives
> 2-3 cloves of fresh garlic, minced
> ½ to 1 cup chopped blanched almonds
> 1 cup stemmed fresh parsley roughly chopped
> 1-2 tsp. grated lemon or orange zest
> 2-3 tbsp. citrus juice (lemon or a combination of lemon and orange)
> 2-3 tbsp. olive oil
> ½ tsp. ground cumin
> ½ tsp. fennel seeds
> ½ tsp. dried thyme

Drain the olives, rinse to reduce saltiness, and pat dry. If you are using salad olives with pimiento, you may want to discard some of the pimiento. If you wish to prepare by hand, simply chop the first four ingredients fine and then mix them with the zest, juice, oil, and seasonings. If you use a food processor, mince the garlic first, then add the parsley and chop that, then add the rest of the ingredients (but watch carefully; it should be somewhat chunky, not like toothpaste.) With either method adjust seasonings and use enough oil to achieve a spreadable consistency. This spread gains in flavor if made ahead of time. Refrigerate if you're making it well in advance, but allow to reach room temperature before serving. Serve with baguette slices or crackers, or spread thinly on bread to make canapes. Garnish with a bit of parsley, some lemon zest and/or pieces of pimiento.

NOTE: This spread may be made with other types of olives, such as Greek Calamatas. Or try oven roasted garlic instead of raw, using a whole head of garlic rather than two cloves. For a traditional tapenade, omit fennel and cumin and substitute four chopped anchovies and 2 tbsp. capers. You can also experiment with nuts other than almonds—for instance pine nuts or walnuts—and with other seasonings, including basil, paprika, black pepper, or finely chopped onion.

7. Ruthie's Crab Dip

Early in our Christmas party existence, my wife cast about for new recipes and found one in an old copy of the Pillsbury Family Cook Book. Mr. Pillsbury served his cold; Ruthie serves it hot. Mr. Pillsbury went easy on the seasonings. Ruthie tosses caution to the wind. It's a real crowd-pleaser, especially when served with toast points on the side made from the Polish light rye.

> 8 ounce can minced clams
> 8 ounce package cream cheese, softened
> 4 tsp. lemon juice
> 1 tsp. salt
> ¼ tsp. cayenne pepper
> 2 tbsp. finely minced onion
> 2 dashes of Louisiana hot sauce
> 2 tsp. prepared horseradish
> paprika and parsley flakes for dusting.

Preheat oven to 350 degrees. Drain clams, reserving liquid. Mix clams with cheese and everything but the paprika. Correct consistency with reserved clam liquid. You don't want it sloppy and you don't want it stiff. Pop in oven and bake until bubbly. Dust with paprika and parsley flakes.

8. Dave's Meatballs

I make these differently every time, so I hesitate to give exact proportions. Three general rules: Lots of filler. Lots of spice.

Make lots and make 'em small, no bigger around then two bits.

> 2 lbs. ground chuck
> 1 lb. ground pork
> 3 eggs
> 4 slices stale bread
> 1 cup half and half
> 1 large onion finely minced or grated
> 1 tsp. poultry seasoning
> 1 tsp. thyme
> 1 tsp. allspice
> 1 tbsp. cinnamon
> salt and pepper to taste
> 1 can of chicken broth
> 1 pint sour cream

Soak bread in half and half until it falls apart. Beat with eggs. Add mixture to meat, onions, and seasonings. Refrigerate for at least one hour. Make a small patty and fry in pan until done. Taste. Correct seasoning. Roll into balls about the size of a quarter. Bake on cookie sheet until done. Cook chicken broth and sour cream together into a sauce. Put meatballs in baking dish, pour over sauce. Serve warm with little roll-ups of lefse. The best commercial lefse to my mind is Countryside, available in quality markets.

9. Dave's Cod Fritters

Here's an old, old-fashioned recipe that belies my Yankee roots. Dried codfish was a staple when I was a kid. It was cheap, it kept well, and the drying process made it tastier than fresh codfish once the dried stuff had been soaked in several baths of fresh water. We ate it creamed on toast, we ate it with fried potatoes and onions. To this day Italians eat it cold in salads, something I don't recommend. You can't find it at every grocery store, but when we moved to River Falls, Merlin the Butcher at Dick's Market was kind enough to order a few boxes of "Atlantic Pearl Salted Cod," which comes in cute wooden boxes. Merlin tells me that other folks in town, once they saw it and remembered it from years back, have begun to buy it, too. If the following recipe ever get out, it will replace the current rage for crabcakes.

> ½ lb. salt cod, soaked according to directions on box
> 1 egg beaten
> 4 tbsps. finely minced onion
> 4 tbsps. finely minced red bell pepper
> 2 tbsps. fresh chopped parsley, preferably flat leaf
> several slices of fresh bread ground in food processor
> vegetable oil for frying

When fillets of cod have been properly soaked and don't taste too salty (don't soak them too long or they won't taste at all!), tear them into tiny pieces. Mix with onion, parsley, and pepper. Add egg and fresh bread crumbs to bind. Refrigerate for one hour. Form into small patties, roll in more fresh bread crumbs. Place on cookie sheet and freeze. When solidly frozen, you can fry them without their falling apart. Heat oil to 350 degrees and fry a few at a time. Serve warm with a sauce of Hellman's mayonnaise to which you've added a dollop of shredded horseradish and a dash of lemon juice.

10. Al Sicherman's Fruit Cake

When it comes to folks who write about food, Al Sicherman of the Minneapolis Star Tribune is right up there with Calvin Trillin, Jeffrey Steingarten, and other nationally known writers who not only like food, but like to have fun with it. Sicherman is a Milwaukee native who often comes to our Christmas parties. During the singalong, his voice soars above others. He's the only person of our acquaintance who knows all the verses to "Good King Wenceslas." One year I said to him, "Al, none of the Christians here know anything further than the first stanza. How come a Jew like you knows them all?" "If you were a Jew living in the neighborhood in Milwaukee where I grew up, you HAD to know all the verses." Here's his excellent fruit cake, distinguished by the fact it contains one pound of ground pork. Have I mentioned that Al is not Orthodox?

> 1 lb. bulk pork sausage, uncooked
> 1 cup raisins
> 1 cup chopped walnuts or pecans
> 1 ½ cups firmly packed brown sugar
> 1 ½ cups granulated sugar
> 2 eggs
> 3 cups all-purpose flour
> 2 tsps. pumpkin pie spice
> 1 ½ tsps. ground ginger
> 1 tsp. baking powder
> 1 cup water and 2 tsp. instant coffee
> 1 tsp. baking soda
> Powdered sugar glaze, pecan halves, holly leaves, and
>   glacé whole cherries for garnish

In a large bowl, mix together sausage, raisins, walnuts, sugars and eggs. Mix flour with pumpkin pie spice, ginger, and baking powder. Stir together water, instant coffee, and baking soda. Add flour mixture and liquid alternately to sausage mixture. Pour into a buttered and flour-dusted 10-inch tube pan or a 12 cup fluted-tube cake pan. Bake in a 350 degree oven for one hour and 25 minutes or until a wooden pick, inserted in the center, comes out clean. (Lightly cover cake with foil if it begins to brown excessively.) Let cool 10 minutes, then turn out onto a rack to cool completely. To serve, paint with glaze, decorate with pecans, holly, and cherries if desired. Cut in 20-25 thin slices.

11. Anne Pederson's Berliner Kranser

When I was a little boy, my mother baked Berliner Kranser for our Christmas festivities. I loved them because they not only tasted good, but they were cute. Mother didn't leave a recipe behind, so I missed them for years, until there arrived in the mail a cookbook published by the Augsburg College Alumni Association board. It's called "From Torsk to Tofu," a takeoff on the late Carl Chrislock's centennial history of Augsburg College, "From Fjord to Freeway," which traced the arrival from Norway of immigrants who wanted to begin a college that ended up on the edge of I-94. It's full of good recipes, many of them Scandinavian, but the one that means the most to me came from Anne Pederson, class of 1932 and a former colleague of mine. Anne never did anything in her long life that was shoddy, so I jumped at her recipe for Berliner Kranser. I'm glad I did.

> ¼ cup sour cream
> 1 cup sugar (more for surface)
> ½ cup softened butter
> 4 egg yolks, beaten (egg whites reserved)
> 2 cups flour
> ¼ tsp. baking soda

Blend sour cream and sugar. Add butter and eggs. Stir in flour and baking soda. Mix thoroughly. Chill. Break off small pieces of dough, roll in 6-inch lengths and shape each into a wreath. Brush with reserved egg white, dust with granulated sugar or green ornamental sugar. Bake in 350 degree oven.

12. Elsie Pirsig's Popcorn Balls

Ruthie used to gnaw on these when she was a little girl in Oak Lawn, Illinois. You probably wouldn't want to serve these at a cocktail party, but why not wrap them in plastic and give them to your guests as party favors to take home to their kids?

Pop enough white popcorn to make 30 balls. Dump it in a basin and shake so "old maids" (is that politically incorrect?)

drop to the bottom. Gingerly remove the corn that is fully popped and place in another bowl. Now assemble.

> 2 cups white sugar
> 2/3 cup water
> 2/3 cup clear corn syrup
> 1 tsp. salt
> 4 tbsp. butter
> 3 tbsp. distilled vinegar

Boil ingredients until a spoon of the mixture forms a soft ball when dropped in cold water. Remove from heat and pour over popped corn, while someone else stirs constantly. Cool a bit and shape into balls. It helps to butter your hands lightly before shaping the hot mixture. Ouch! (If you're richer than Elsie was, it wouldn't hurt to throw a tin of redskin peanuts into the mixture.)

13. Ruth's Incredibily Fussy Stuffed Popovers

Although, these hors d'ouevres are very delicious, I wouldn't make them if they gave me the oil fields of Saudi Arabia, lock stock and barrel. But it's just the sort of thing Ruth loves to do. I think it's the Ph.D. in her, a tendency to make a thing or an idea as complicated as possible.

> ¼ lb. smoked salmon, flaked
> 1 jar of Romanoff black caviar
> 1 package of cream cheese
> ½ pt. sour cream
> 2 tbsp. finely minced onion
> freshly squeezed lemon juice
> sprigs of fresh dillweed
> 1 batch of small popovers, 1 ½ inches

Mix cream cheese, sour cream, onion, lemon juice. Cut tops off popovers. Reserve. Carefully pick out unbaked dough inside of the popovers. Just before serving put dabs of cream cheese mixture in each popover, followed by salmon, followed by a dab of caviar. Top with a tiny sprig of dill. Top with reserved popover tops. Serve at once. See what I mean?

14. Cheapskate Caviar: Its Care and Serving

Legend has it that gourmet/travel writer Lucius Beebe was a caviar aficionado and that he always carried a tiny gold ball, no bigger than a BB. When his iced Beluga caviar was brought to his table, out came the tiny ball, which he dropped on the fish eggs. If it did not sink to the bottom immediately, he'd send the caviar back. Ruth and I don't serve that sort of caviar. We're partial to Romanoff, the cheap stuff, which is bottled in St. Louis Park, Minnesota, a long way from the Caspian Sea. You could drop the ball bearing out of Farmall Super M and it wouldn't sink to the bottom of Romanoff, which is made of eggs from the Lumpfish (ugh!). Still, it's pretty good stuff if you know how to serve it. When I unscrew the cap of the little jar, I squeeze a bit of lemon juice onto the eggs, which can be either red or black. Then I make a spread of cream cheese, lemon juice, sour cream, and minced onion. And I spread it out on a small platter and refrigerate. When the cheese is set, I dump the fish eggs into the middle of the cheese and spread around, leaving at least an inch of cheese border. The border I garnish with grated hard-boiled egg and minced fresh dill. I serve with toast points.   If guests don't eat it all, I moosh everything together and make a sandwich to send with Ruth to school the next day.

15. Uncle Clarence Schwarz's Pfefferneuse

Ruth always liked her Uncle Clarence's pfefferneuse, or "peppernuts" better than her own mother's. But when we phoned to get the recipe, Uncle Clarence said it wasn't his recipe at all, but came from his and Elsie's mother, Lena Schwarz, born in Feuchtwangen, Bavaria, and settled in Lakota,

Iowa. We'll still call it Uncle Clarence's—and hope that Elsie isn't reading this in that Big Kitchen in the Sky.

½ cup REAL sour cream (not cultured)
¾ cup oleo margarine (butter does not work in this recipe)
1 cup sugar
4 cups sifted flour
1 egg
½ tsp. pepper ("pfeffer")
1 tsp. soda
½ tsp. salt
½ tsp. vanilla extract
2 tbsp. anise seed.

Make real sour cream by putting ½ cup half & half outside the fridge for a day. Mix it with other ingredients and chill overnight. Roll handsfull of dough into cigar-sized pieces and cut ¾ inch pieces off them. Then roll each piece into a round "nut" (neusse). Nuts should be acorn size. Place on a sprayed cookie sheet and pop into 350 degree oven for about 20 minutes, or until "nice and brown," according to Aunt Verna, Clarence's wife.

CHAPTER X

CODA

We end in joy.
—Theodore Roethke

I hope this little book has been as much fun for you to read as it was for me to write. But we've got to stop somewhere. So this is it. To show my appreciation, we'll close with ALL of the stanzas of "Good King Wenceslas," just in case you ever end up at a Christmas party standing next to Al Sicherman, the very model of a culturally diverse gentleman.

> Good King Wenceslas looked out
> On the Feast of Stephen,
> When the snow lay 'round about
> Deep and crisp and even.
> Brightly shone the moon that night,
> Though the frost was cruel,
> When a poor man came in sight,
> Gath'ring winter fuel.
>
> "Hither, page, and stand by me!
> If thou hast heard telling,
> Yonder peasant—who is he?
> Where and what his dwelling?"

"Sire, he lives a good league hence,
Underneath the mountain,
Right against the forest fence
By Saint Agnes' fountain."

"Bring me flesh and bring me wine!
Bring me pine-logs hither!
Thou and I will see him dine
When we bear them thither!"
Page and monarch, forth they went;
Forth they went together,
Through the rude wind's wild lament
And the bitter weather.

"Sire, the night grows darker now,
And the wind blows stronger.
Fails my heart—I know not how
I can go much longer!"
"Mark my footsteps, my good page,
Tread thou in them boldly.
Thou shall feel this winter's rage
Freeze thy blood less coldly."

In his master's steps he trod,
Where the snow lay dinted.
Heat was in the very sod
Which the saint had printed.
Therefore, Christian men, be sure,
Wealth or rank possessing,
Ye who now will bless the poor
Shall yourselves find blessing.

About the Author:

After many years teaching British literature at colleges and universities in the Midwest, Dave Wood began a second career as a columnist for the Minneapolis Tribune and for several midwestern magazines, including Wisconsin Trails and Grit, the national family magazine.

He is the author of several books. In 1974 and 1999, he received the first place award from the Wisconsin Newspaper Association for Best Local Column. He is a past vice-president of the National Book Critics Circle and writes a weekly syndicated column, "Dave Wood's Book Report." He lives with his wife, Ruth Pirsig Wood, in River Falls, Wisconsin.

Other Books by Dave Wood

Wisconsin Life Trip
Wisconsin Prairie Diary
Telling Tales Out of School
My Mother the Arsonist
The Anderson Chronicles (with Richard Nelson)